WRESTLING WITH GOD
Contradiction or Confrontation –
the Dichotomy of God

BY DARIN JONES

xulon
PRESS

Wrestling With God
Contradiction or Confrontation - the Dichotomy of God
by Darin Jones

Printed in the United States of America
Edited by Xulon Press

Photography:
Nicole Isaacson Newton
Princeton, IL 61356
815.878.6406
www.nicoleisaacsonphotography.com

ISBN 9781498414180

www.xulonpress.com

FOREWORD

—◦◦◦◦—

Our Dichotomous God

Ever wonder sometimes why God doesn't just split the skies and with a Cecil B. DeMille effect (a la *Transformers 3* technology), suddenly just appear? BAM!! Why doesn't He just show up and rock everybody's world – literally – with simply His presence, and cause all mankind to fall to our knees, and without a shadow of a doubt, once and for all acknowledge that, "Yep, there He is; there is God!"?

It's a good question. Some say He does and we are so busy, preoccupied, or cynical that we just don't see it. Why then is He so private about it? Why so subtle? He wasn't private about Mount Sinai. He wasn't subtle about Sodom and Gomorrah. He was pretty out there in front with Lazarus and when he fed the 5,000! But ever since Jesus told the fellas, "I'm going, but

I'll send someone to help you," (John 16:5-7, para-phrasing) we've been scratching our heads and asking, "Is that You?"

On one hand, you would think that the Almighty Creator of the universe would want to make it simple for us to walk right up to Him. After all, wasn't that part of the idea of Jesus? On the other hand, the complexity of human reasoning and understanding, the intertwining of our emotions with logic and affection and feeling, calls for answers at every level! Doesn't it? Simple answers don't seem to satisfy complex thinkers. Complex solutions confound the simple. So which is it – is God so complex that we just can't figure it out, or is He so simple that He's been right there in front of our noses all this time and we've just not seen Him!?

Yes!

Not a very satisfying answer, huh? Leaves you going back and forth a bit, doesn't it? When you are expecting some relief to the angst of dealing with the logical struggle rolling around in your head, and all you get is an answer like "yes," it can very well be a bit discouraging, can't it? Because we want it simple and plain. The problem is, if we get that answer, whether it rocks our world or not, we immediately move on, and our engagement, the wrestling match, is over. Not unlike a three-year-old at his first big birthday party. Lots of friends and the stack of gifts have his eyes bulging. As he tears through the wrapping of each gift, no matter how grand or awesome the gift–no matter that it was the very thing that he desired (and begged for) the most above all else–he casts it aside to continue the assault on the pile of gifts. He moves on. And so do we. Even if we get the answer we were looking for, even if we witness the miracle, we do the same thing! We move on.

One of the most terrifying thoughts that I have carried since childhood is this: What comes after God? The specter of eternity! Okay, so we die and go to heaven and hang out for quite some time…. Sooooo, then what? What is there beyond God? In the vast expanse that is everything, what more is there? Because there has to be more, right? What is around, behind, below, above God? Like that three-year-old, I'm looking for more! In my heart of hearts, I know He is there, but in my small mind I cannot conceive of the space that He operates in — that dimension outside of time!!

Stay with me now – what comes after Him? I don't know! And guess what!? That is a good thing! I am not going to know – possibly ever! Because if we could come to the end of God, then we, like Lucifer, would try to claim His place. Thinking we had arrived at some vista or self-important level of understanding, the wrestling match would end—at least in our minds it would. We so easily begin to think more highly of ourselves than we ought! One thing is for sure though: there *is* more.

"How do you know?" you say. Here is the simple answer: because I love! Not like hamburgers or my favorite shirt. Not that kind of love. But I love with a feeling and emotion that would cast all caution and self-preservation aside and utterly sacrifice my life (hardly a survival-of-the-fittest instinct) for several people who are very close to me! THAT kind of love!! So then, where does that kind of affection come from? It's not natural, but it is definitely real. Most any parent can attest to this.

In his book on auditioning for Broadway, director Michael Shurtleff tells actors to consider every scene in a play a "love scene." It's not that every scene is romantic. But every scene has emotion, and our core emotion is love. "The desire for love, to give it or receive it... is the chief propellant in human beings," wrote Shurtleff. "An actor had best learn that."[1] And so should we.

All right, all right, all right, so He is there! And He is love. What's the point, and what are we supposed to do with that?

Well, most believe we were made for the purpose of bringing Him acclaim, or "for His glory." And we were! We were the climax of His creation–His magnum opus. He says so. But somehow, we still fall short. Because we are such knuckleheads! Okay, let's be honest. We bugger things up pretty well when left to our own devices! Read the paper lately? But I believe that our Creator was so, well, creative, that He built into us an insatiable drive, a curiosity, to know and see and understand more! And there is more! Unlimited exploration, unending adventure, answers that breed bigger questions, vistas, realms, and kingdoms to experience! Like a computer geek touring Apple's R&D lab! Like that three-year-old at Toys-R-Us! But for any of the thrill to be possible, the toys are not just laid neatly out on the table. We have to contend for them. We have to wrestle!

Jacob feared for his life. He had cheated his brother of his birthright — which would be tantamount to a hefty inheritance. And by the way, his big brother was the large, burly, outdoorsy type that could field dress a deer in sixty seconds! So you can imagine what he might do to his lying, cheating, fair-skinned little brother! Jacob had run off to his family's home of origin and had become wealthy and influential himself. But he had gotten sideways with his father-in-law playing the gotcha-last game of who can fool whom out of the family fortune, and again had to run away back to daddy, back to his hometown. Problem was, big brother was back there! Any hope of crawling back home undetected and quietly setting up camp without big brother finding out was lost when one of his messengers — who was sent ahead to kiss up to his brother if he saw him — returned to tell Jacob that not only was Esau coming to meet him, but he was bringing 400 men with him!!

So Jacob was significantly fearful and trying to figure his way out of this predicament. He had done well with the turn-and-run strategy in the past. But this time, he had to face his issue. He had to face his brother whom he cheated — badly! As if the running away strategy from before hadn't been bad enough, knowing he would eventually have to face his brother, he sent three different messengers with loads of cattle and sheep, each with instructions to suck up to his brother and offer the livestock as gifts so that Esau wouldn't kill him!

The night before the climactic meeting, he sent his procession of wives, children, servants and animals across the river in the direction of his brother while he waited — alone — on the near side, to contemplate his fate. Not exactly the selfless leader that you would expect the patriarch of Israel to be! As he no doubt contemplated turning tail and running away (again) versus facing the fate that God had instructed him to go and face, a man stepped from the shadows. Scripture gives no great detail of what ensued next. But when Jacob locked eyes with Him, it was clearly "go time"! A physical match broke out that was a tangible mirror image of the internal struggle that Jacob had been dealing with all along.

Much of what we cannot see, touch, or audibly hear has an absolute physical component. A "cold chill" runs up your spine when a realized fear grips you. A "warm rush" floods your chest when the object of your affection suddenly proclaims his/her affections for you. A "hot flash" of sudden panic overcomes you when that person you were "just talking about" steps from around the corner where they have been listening to everything you just said. You cannot see a spiritual response – but you feel it!

Jacob had been wrestling with God ever since He told him to go back home. Jacob could go anywhere. He had a handful of wives, a bunch of sons, lots of cattle and sheep and servants. He could go set himself up anywhere he liked and he would be just fine. But no, God told him he had to go back home – where he didn't really want to go. The two men tussled through the night. "*Through the night*," the scripture says! Had they been trying to kill one another, scripture might have described the encounter as a battle, or a fight, or something more contentious than a "wrestle." In Jacob's mind, if he could at least hold on and not give in, he might just survive the following day. At some point in the struggle, consciously or unconsciously, something in Jacob's mind clicked! "I am not winning, but I am not losing either. This is not just a man! God is contending with me!" Jacob's motivation suddenly turned from trying to overcome the man, to trying just to hold on to the man for the same prize that he had cheated his brother and risked his life for – a blessing.

Man, those blessings must have had some crazy huge value in those days! Why don't they now? Or do they, but we ignore them, don't believe, or just don't know it? The sovereign God of the universe, contending with a human, His creation? As the story goes, the man – God – saw that He could not overcome Jacob, so He touched him on the hip and dislocated it....

Think about that for just a minute!

1) God could not overcome a human? I don't think so. But that is what the scripture says. What then does it mean? If God were a disengaged, unapproachable

deity, then of course, anyone who dared to approach, question, or challenge Him would be crushed! BUT, if God really is interpersonal, feeling, caring, and wildly risk-taking, He may just choose to wrestle with us!

2) Why the struggle? Why not just deliver the message – oh, I don't know, on stone tablets, written in the sky, or through one of his cows or donkeys telling him in God-like-all-powerful fashion, and be done with it? Why entangle Himself with a human? Particularly a messed-up, self-seeking human like Jacob at this point? This begs the question, "What was it about Jacob that drew the Almighty God of everything to engage him in this way?"

The outcome of the scrap tells the story. Jacob was sincerely, wholeheartedly, and humbly contending for God. Something inside of him, you could say his heart, was desperately seeking help, seeking God. He had come to the end of himself and had no place to turn but to God. At that point, the point of our complete surrender, God jumps in! But rather than crush Jacob, God engages him, He wrestles.

If you don't have a brother, you may not get this. I suppose any sibling would do, regardless of sex. But the illustration – and therefore the understanding – is much clearer in the context of a brother. If you have ever gotten that look from your brother in a moment of great tension and yet absolute clarity, then you understand the words, "Go time!" Usually the words are not even necessary, because at that point, the time for words has passed. What essentially happens during these bouts? I remember being so angry with my brother. He didn't respect me. He thought he was my boss. He had the nerve to think I was just a kid. He thought he was so tough! Although respect, courtesy, and/or pecking order are usually part of the cause, the struggle is ultimately for control!

The confrontation always ended in one of two ways. I'd pick myself up off the floor and snap, "You big jerk!" over my shoulder, walking away, or we'd both collapse winded and spent, trying to remember the ridiculous reason for the whole thing. In either case, the outcome was a clearer understanding of where my brother and I stood. And so it is with the God of the universe. Some may find it hard to grasp that the Almighty would be at all concerned with knowing me intimately. After all, He created me, so doesn't He already know me pretty well? Of course, but in yet another display of overtly human emotion, He implores us continually to "come" to Him (Matthew 11:28) for rest from trials and difficulties and for a relationship that changes everything and gives life! As wonderfully simple as that should be, the trouble is, we – like Jacob – want the blessing, and also control. Of course we cannot have both. So when we whole-heartedly finally come to Him, entreating Him for this blessing, yet on our terms, it is then that He may just choose to wrestle. And that means tension.

Ever notice the tension that is built into the Word of God? In Deuteronomy He commands, "Thou shalt not kill." But later in 1 Samuel He commands Saul to "completely destroy the entire Amalekite nation – men, women, children, babies, cattle, sheep, goats, camels, and donkeys." In fact, there is a lot of killin' going on all through the Old Testament. David Jeremiah says it this way:

> God by His Holy Spirit has built tension into His Word in a magnificent way so that we never go off in any direction too far. The truth is held together in a kind of insoluble relationship so that we are kept in the right place. For instance, if I am only told that God is my father, then I have a tendency to move over into that realm of flippancy, that kind of extra-familiarity, the slanguage that is often built up around religion and a personal relationship with the father, i.e. 'the Big Guy', or 'the Man Upstairs'. But we are reminded that

He is '...our Father who art in heaven.' On one
hand He is my father, on the other hand He
dwells in heaven.[2]

He is the Almighty, the Sovereign Lord, Lord
of Heaven and Earth, His Majesty, King of Kings!
And He is my Father, Abba, Daddy. He is unimaginable, unfathomable! Yet He is as approachable as
a gentle, loving father. Again, why the tension? In
the following chapters, I hope to run headlong into
that tension that either gives us pause or causes us
to doubt—sometimes even the existence of God, and
not just His presence. At the same time, I'd like to
address those who might look only at the surface of
what would appear to be contradictions, and not fully
consider that there may be something more going on
in texts like Proverbs 26:4-5 (NASB): *Do not answer
a fool according to his folly, Or you will also be like
him. Answer a fool as his folly deserves, That he not
be wise in his own eyes.* (Interesting that these verses
would be used in a section dealing with fools.) At
www.atheism.about.com, Austin Cline writes:

Believers argue that contradictions are only
"alleged" and that all alleged contradictions
can be resolved or harmonized. In some cases

it is true that contradictions or inconsistencies can be resolved, but only at a cost that believers shouldn't want to pay: by adding to the text, by ignoring key aspects of the text, or by developing novel, complex interpretations of a text that is supposed to be simply taken at face value rather than interpreted. A perfect, omnipotent, omniscient God should be able to cause to exist a text which doesn't require acrobatics and desperate rationalizations to make sense of it.

I get where Austin is coming from, but let's take a step back for just one moment, inject some honest introspection, and ask ourselves if there couldn't be more to what we believe – or do not believe – about God. All of scripture is useful for instruction, even at face value! Stoning your disobedient kids (Deuteronomy 21:18-21) is especially useful to discuss with your unruly son! But seriously, do you not think that there is something more going on in that verse beyond an edict to kill your kid for not taking out the trash? I am no theologian. Maybe I've just lived long enough now to be fed up with all the nonsense and would like to finally see folks make an honest assessment of this number one, bestselling book *of all time*, and its Author. For over 2,000 years, we have read and studied and dissected and translated the words given to us in the Bible – God's words. Denominations, orders, factions, and worse, religious cults and nut-job activist groups have formed behind the words of that book. Critics (like Austin) mock apparent contradictions, scholars argue literal vs. figurative interpretation, and those in the middle struggle for a practical application to their Monday morning grind.

Why is so much left for us to figure out? How could something so important be left for argument? At the core of all we know and believe, the filter of all of our life's experiences is our conscience, our spirit, our gut – our heart! And THAT is what the God of the universe is chiefly interested in! So in giving us evidence, setting an example, showing us part but not all, and then stepping back to allow us to draw our own conclusions – which we argue and bicker about – He exposes what is behind all that we say and do. He exposes our heart.

Not that I could ever completely define or explain God, or His reasons for doing things like He does, but my hope is to at least bring some pause, maybe some understanding, or at least a little peace of mind to the things of God that make us go, "Huh?" Those things I call God's dichotomy.

Dichotomy is Difficulty

Two seemingly opposite truths or instructions – apparent contradictions that cause us to struggle with the meaning behind the words. This is a dichotomy. But with Jehovah, the struggle is the point. Yes, both can be true, but to get there, to understand more completely, you have to struggle with apparent warring instructions. You have to get to the heart that is behind the words! God does not just want us to understand and perform according to His instructions. He wants us to actually feel what He feels about a particular circumstance or principle. He wants us to have a fuller, deeper understanding – one that brings us into partnership with Him in desiring what He desires.

I watched a doctor once who was training a resident on a procedure – an actual procedure in an operating room (that's how they learn). So, the resident is tentative and is dissecting through some tissue very near the heart. There appears to be a somewhat large blood vessel very close to where he is dissecting. The doctor who is instructing him is all over him about staying near and working on the vessel and not beside it or around it. Clearly, the resident understands why the dissection is necessary. He is trying to free up several vessels leading to a section of the lung so that he can tie them off and remove that section. But he is hesitant. Let me just state the obvious. Vessels near the heart are scary! They are big, under a significant amount of pressure, and if you nick one, you are in deep... well, you are in big trouble!

So the resident is nervously working to one side or the other. The doc keeps correcting him and telling him to stay in the middle, to pick up small bites of the tissue with one instrument and tease or dissect through it with the other instrument. The resident is sweating, his hands move more slowly with each stroke. Two more times the doc yells at him and tells him, "Not over there, you need to be working right THERE!" pointing to the center of the giant menacing vessel.

"But...." the resident pleads.

"THERE!" the doc insists one more time.

Finally, with one more stroke – the stroke that everyone else in the room thought would put us knee-deep in blood – a sheath surrounding a bundle of vessels opens up and several vessels that were held together by the covering tissue spring into view, separate and distinct. Now the resident understands more completely – not only the location and position of the multiple vessels, but the difficulty in identifying them, the care necessary for uncovering them, the importance of the experience, and the proper regard for working in such a space. He has a deeper understanding. And because of the struggle, he will never forget!

"Thou shalt not kill." (Exodus 20:13 KJV)

Versus

"Now go and completely destroy the entire Amalekite nation – men, women, children, babies, cattle, sheep, goats, camels, and donkeys." (1 Samuel 15:3 NLT)

Chapter 1

KILL OR BE KILLED

S keptics bark about this apparent disregard for human life from a supposedly loving God. But aren't these the same people who think human life was just an accident? If that were the case, then what would be so sacred about it that they would criticize how it was handled – or ended? The hypocrisy is rich! The fact that anyone would criticize anything as "unjust" begs the question, "Who is the judge of what is just?" Mankind? Seriously? You can't get two people from even similar backgrounds to agree on a principle as basic as life (as in the death penalty, abortion, and suicide), so good luck finding a consensus among any people group on the universality of any law or practice!

Why do you think our society has become so litigious and lawyers so numerous? Law itself is reinterpreted daily in our courts. You cannot have morality or justice if there is no universal judge or giver of that law in the first place! But, I digress.

As most of you already know, there is a distinction between the "kill" of Exodus 20 and the "destroy" of 1 Samuel 15. Exodus 20 is the commandment given to Moses, and is more accurately translated "commit murder," which any good lawyer would tell you involves malice and forethought. Murder is a planned, intentional taking of another life for, let's say, NOT so honorable reasons.

Most all of the killing we see throughout the Bible, particularly in the Old Testament, had a lot to do with judgment. If God is just, and demands justice, then why do we rail against the "utter destruction" of a bunch of people who sacrifice their own babies, rape, steal, and destroy for their own pleasure? Face it, the world was a nasty place when people were left without any real standard for behavior, but only did what seemed best to them! All that the Ten Commandments did was point out how screwed up we really were – or are. People hated Israel all the more because of the "rules" they imposed, and just wrote them off – like the world does now to people who try to follow the rules – as religious freaks!

Funny how nobody argues the lying, stealing, murdering, or adultery commands, but we seem to get hung up on the "no other gods," "God's name in vain," "Sabbath day," and "no idols" commands! It's kind of an all-or-nothing deal. We really do not get to choose which ones work best for us and cast the others aside. They either all have validity and authority, or none of them do. Hmm.

Why then the seismic shift when we cross over from Old Testament to New? Seems like all the fighting stops. We no longer hear of wars, takeovers, mass killings, countries being overthrown, etc. Well, one reason is that Rome dominated the world at that particular time, so little besides Rome's atrocities are heard of. To be sure, there was still plenty of killing going on, and wars had never ceased. But the narrative is significantly less bloody – until, that is, the one guy who taught about turning the other cheek and loving your enemies called out the power brokers of His day and threatened to expose them for the hypocrites that they were. He said if you call your brother an idiot, you might as well have just stuck a knife in him! But who could ever resist uttering those words to your dingbat brother, especially when he has demonstrated all of the qualifications of an "idiot"? So, you have to ask, "What did He mean by that?" The tricky

23

part is, sometimes He means just what it says, and other times He is clearly digging at something deeper.

Of all the sources that I have read on killing in the Bible, "Mr. Dale" at *answers.yahoo.com* (of all places) offers what I think was one of the most interesting answers:

> Thou shalt not Murder is more accurate [a translation of Exodus 20:13].
>
> The descendants of Cain were Extremely Violent and Evil. They were the worst kinds of people ever known, like they were all demon possessed. Remember, 1/3 of all the angels fell and these angels were not just sitting around hoping one or two people were going to accept them. These were entire cities and nations that were out to kill God's people. God used 300 men with Gideon to kill the thousands that were about to slaughter God's people.
>
> Keep in mind, Jesus was promised as the Messiah and God's hand was on the descendants of Adam through David to keep them safe and out of harm's way.
>
> Many times, [by the way], God's people tried to make nice with them, but the descendants of Cain wanted NO peace, only war. So, what

was left to do? Either, kill (self defense) or be killed (without a reason).
Today we call it a preemptive strike. It's justifiable. The US is doing it right now!
Neither God, nor the US condones the taking of human life. However, both command it in the laws that govern us.

I spent six years in the military as a field artillery officer. Prior to that, I attended the U.S. Military Academy for four years. During my first (plebe) year at the Academy, I had come home for Christmas and attended a service at a small church where my brother was an interim pastor. After the service, my brother and I met with some of the congregation who had stayed after to ask questions of my brother and me as a kind of "point-counterpoint" exchange. The question was asked, "How do you feel about being in the business of killing people while your brother here is in the business of saving them?"

It was a question I had wrestled with even before deciding (at the ripe age of eighteen) to attend West Point. I had studied all of the major world wars in junior high and high school well enough to have a cursory knowledge of their origins and the reasoning behind our involvement. I think – at least at the time when I was growing up – we may have had a tendency to over-romanticize war, particularly as time had passed and our memories of them had become softened by a longer-distance perspective. We look back and think only of the glories and the great lessons that were learned and forget about the awfulness of the whole thing. Nevertheless, the United States does not engage in war for no purpose, or for reasons that are less than honorable. Typically, the U.S. engages in aiding a smaller, less equipped people who seek self-governance (democracy), defending those whose lives have been infringed upon, or defending our own land and people. Sure, we can argue all day about the political ramifications of campaigns like Vietnam, but as a general rule, the Constitution grants only Congress (a large group of people who are accountable to us and to one another) and no individual the ability to declare war. I have a fair amount of confidence in "the counsel of many." (Proverbs 11:14; 15:22)

Our bottom line, historically, has been this: big (bad) country invades or attacks smaller (innocent) country, we come to the aid (good) of the smaller country. We seek justice. Not unlike a police officer who, by his presence, elicits either comfort in knowing that someone has got your back, or fear, because you may be doing something wrong (bad)! As an instrument of that justice, at some level a soldier must place himself (or herself), his service, and indeed his life under the authority of another. How any particular operation is carried out may call upon his better judgment, but the decision to go to war, and the belief in the veracity of the campaign cannot be questioned. If this grates on you, then you have authority issues. Read Romans 13:1-7, Hebrews 13:17, Titus 3:1, 1 Peter 2:13, and others, and repent. So, if my cause is just, then the taking of human life in the course of that cause is – as in 1 Samuel 15 – justified. My motivation is not to mindlessly kill a human being because I have the means and a cause. I am driven by justice and the decisions of commanders whom God Himself has placed over me. The last verse of our national anthem puts it like this:

O thus be it ever, when freemen shall stand
Between their loved home and the war's desolation.
Blest with vict'ry and peace, may the Heav'n rescued land
Praise the Power that hath made and preserved us a nation!
Then conquer we must, when our cause it is just,
And this be our motto: "In God is our trust."

And the star-spangled banner in triumph shall wave
O'er the land of the free and the home of the brave!³

Incidentally, every soldier on the battlefield has accepted the cost that may be exacted of him. We go into battle with the expectation that our life is at risk for the cause for which we are fighting. If we had no conviction about our cause, we would not be there in the first place. We consider it no great travesty or breach of our beliefs that our life on this earth, or that of our enemy, may end on that day. We likewise make the assumption that the enemy has accepted these facts. So, in the end, I will back the strength of my convictions with my life. To do otherwise would seem hypocritical. John (the Baptist) did not instruct the Roman soldiers to put down their weapons and walk off the job. He told them to act justly. (Luke 3:14)

Few think of Abraham as a "man of war;" however, Genesis 14 shows he was one. As soon as he heard that his relative, Lot, was a captive, Abraham armed all his trained men and waged war on Lot's captors. The Bible does not record that God told Abraham to go to war nor does it indicate Abraham made any effort to consult God to see "if it was God's will" that he wage war. Abraham "walked with God" and he already knew God's will enough to know that God would allow him to go to war under such circumstances. The fact that Abraham had sufficient weapons in his encampment to quickly arm 318 servants for war (Genesis 14:14) indicates that while Abraham had "faith in God," he also traveled with an arsenal of weapons! Abraham saw no conflict between being "a man of faith," and also being "a man of war" when circumstances required him to be one. Upon His return, will Jesus meekly "forgive all his enemies" and "turn the other cheek" to those who oppose His rule? Not at all! He will wage war upon them and slaughter them (Luke 19:27, Revelation 14:14-20, etc.)![4]

No, I do not believe that being a follower of Christ necessitates that you be a conscientious objector to war, but neither should we be too eager to engage in it. Again, the question remains: What is in your heart? Just enough instruction is given in scripture to set a precedent, and Jesus' example gives us just enough pause that we cannot simply answer the killing question off the cuff. We have to look hard at our own motivation. We have to wrestle.

"Therefore, My dear friends, as you have always obeyed –not only in my presence, but now much more in my absence – continue to work out your salvation with fear and trembling…" (Philippians 2:12)

Versus

"…for it is God who works in you to will and to act in order to fulfill His good purpose." (Philippians 2:13)

Chapter 2

"EVERYBODY'S WORKING FOR THE WEEKEND"[5]

W ow, one verse right after the other that would appear to go in opposite directions! I'm pretty sure He does this on purpose. Here is what looks like a boldface contradiction in back to back verses. You work or God works? Are we supposed to work at it or not? "It" being our salvation, our relationship with God, and our understanding of what He wants us to do. On one end of the spectrum there are those who lean more toward the "...what will be will be and there is nothing you can do about it..." mindset, who think that any amount of effort on our part to seek God is vanity and useless chasing after the wind. Then on the other end of that spectrum there are those who just cannot do enough; who stress about everything from what they will wear to work that day to an almost moment-by-moment confession for every sin committed since childhood, and a non-stop list of things that they are doing for God! They busy themselves with multiple levels of tasks for the church or for friends, in a kind of feigned dedication to "kingdom works."

We like to be busy, don't we (talk to Martha—Luke 10:38-42)? The thinking goes something like this: "If I am very busy, then that means that I have an important job with important things that need to get done—right away, because they are important things and I am the only important one who can do them correctly because I am just that good, and, well, if I don't get these very important things done, then the world just may stop turning!" I am, of course, being facetious, but you get the point. We like busy! On balance, labor is meaningful and it does have value. Sure, God could have done a fine job watching over the garden Himself, but He gave that job to Adam to help him see his value and importance—and truthfully, I'm sure he also needed something to keep him occupied and out of trouble...!

So the work was given by God. It is a good thing. But just like so many of us who have made work the main thing, we likewise tend to make our works for God central to our self-felt value to God.

That is a mistake! But you see how easily we slide from *work* value to *works* value? I am with James (James 2:17): faith without works is useless. But that internal struggle for greater significance presses me to do more – more good things make me even better, right? Better than that guy over there! Kind of like the ridiculous logic of, "...if a little fertilizer is good, then piling it on the yard is better, right...?" Or, "...if a little cold medicine is good, then I should pound the whole bottle and that will be even better – because my cold is really bad...!?" We just have this crazy human tendency to overdo it with the things that we think we can manage because it is so hard to just accept the things that we can't!

Why is a healthy balance so difficult to achieve? I love my kids because they are my children – flesh of my flesh. Yeah, it's nice when they do good things to show their regard for me, but it would be heartbreaking to me to hear them say something like, "Look, Daddy, I cleaned my room – so do you *really* love me now?" Or, "Hey, I mowed the lawn *and* took the garbage out, and she – your other daughter – well, ha, she only vacuumed the living room!" That's great honey, but I will never love you or her any less. And so, again, our tendency then is to fly off the handle in the other direction and never clean our room – because He just said it would not earn me more love, right?

We cannot earn the love of a (the) father, but that does not mean that we can flatly disobey what we know are the things He wants us to do and not expect a reprimand. Does God punish? He is called FATHER – what do you think? Like everything else that we would tend to argue about, this fleshes out our heart. What is behind the works? Is it a regard and a desire to demonstrate my affection and gratitude? Is it love? Or is it an attempt to justify myself or just get what I want – credit and acclaim for my hard work?! I don't mean to keep going in such circles here, but you see that finding a balance, not flying off the handle in either direction, is the (sometimes elusive) goal.

We honestly do not do this naturally. Circumstances come at us – the car breaks down and now you need a new alternator, *cough, cough!* You can think of at least fifty other good uses for the $400! You could do it yourself to save some cash, but if you are not mechanically inclined, this will cost you far more in terms of lost time and gray hair than the $400. Or you could take it to a dealer who makes the model you own, and there may be an up-charge for the newer parts and the dealership's hours. Or you could take it to your friend who is a mechanic, who will probably save you some money. The part will not be new, but it will work. Ah, the choices life throws at us! Question: Is God concerned with a decision like this? I mean, really, is He all that concerned with what kind of alternator gets put in our car? Is He concerned with where we buy our clothes, either at a department store, or custom tailored from an upscale specialty store?

Decisions like these and the thought process that is behind them do reveal something about us. They reveal what is going on inside! Is my intent in going to the dealership, or the tailor, just a bent to get the best money can buy—because I have the money? Or is it because I have been bitten by second-hand parts before, and I just feel like it's worth the extra money if it will last longer? Is the idea of going to my buddy the mechanic simply an attempt to save my money with the cheapest option on the table? Or am I trying to be wise with the money that I have been given, and trusting that the cheaper option will be sufficient? Motivation is everything! Believe me, I have been on both ends of that spectrum and paid top dollar for tailored pants that felt and looked great, but fell apart in short order. And I found a great pair of pants off the rack that have fit great and lasted for years! I've gotten burned by my own selfish desire to hold on tight-fisted to MY money (which ultimately it is not), and limp the car along for another 3,000 miles on bald tires and a failing suspension, only to pay extra to have the car towed and nearly lose my life on the highway!

That's the long way around of saying, "YES," ultimately He is concerned with every miniscule decision you make! Luke 12:7 says, "…even the hairs on your head are numbered." In saying something like that, do you get the idea that He is interested in the details!? Why else would He say something as expressive and detailed as that? I live in the country, and the other day, driving into town, a bird pinged off my windshield after flying into the road instead away from it – country birds are just a little slower. And I thought to myself, God knows that bird, and is concerned even about its demise! Honestly, having just paid off the repairs on my car for the jumbo-sized raccoon that ran out in front of me last fall, my first reaction was, "Stupid bird – get out of the way!" Second thought was 'God knows that bird'…. But here is a mind blower: Could that bird's life have been all about teaching me – and by extension you – this simple truth, that God IS concerned about our smallest decision, our every thought, the hairs on our head, and many sparrows?!

So how far do I take this? What if I stopped and prayed about every little decision throughout the day?

Are you kidding me? I'd never get anything done! That is, if by praying you mean getting down on my knees and saying a lot of thees and thous and working myself into a self-deprecating fit. Well, yes, that could take a while. But, if I'm just talking about a conversation – which comes naturally if I am in a real relationship with Him – then my best prayer is only a moment's hesitation, an inaudible "What do you think, Lord?" and off we go! However, if the issue or question at hand is something that I know He would not be altogether pleased with, yet I am determined to have it/do it/want it, then the wrestling match is "on"! I can go back and forth with God all day long in an attempt to justify why I don't do what I know needs to be done. I will never win that argument, but the exchange *will* bring me closer to Him! Do you see it?

I think He sometimes leaves things out there simply *because* He wants that exchange. We are descendents of Adam! We are going to screw up some things! I almost wonder if this wasn't by design, "In this life you will have trouble" (John 16:33). So, back to the original question: works or no works? As before, the answer is "Yes!" We have to be honest about where that fine line exists between puffing myself up and taking action on my beliefs. Am I doing things for the outward appearance, to look good? Or am I doing

37

those things out of love and appreciation for the life I've been given and the relationship I have with the one who gave it to me?

Work as though you were putting everything on the line for a coach/ mentor/friend who had invested heavily in you, and whom you trust, honor, and respect implicitly. And work as though that coach/ mentor/friend were also your father who you know beyond a shadow of any doubt loves you no matter what. It sets us at ease and frees us to work our best when we know that our efforts will be appreciated and rewarded. Knowing that coach/mentor/friend really is looking out for us and really wants us to succeed completely changes the dynamic of our work. Though most work places don't exactly work that way, that's how 'works' were meant to be, an expression of our motivation simply to return that love and respect. Let THAT drive you to give only your best! It is so settling for the mind to know that our best efforts, whether they hit the mark or not, will be appreciated and accepted. As my beloved high school football coach always said, "Play as hard as you can for as long as you can and let the chips fall where they may!" The pressure to perform is gone! It's just assumed that you are giving it your best shot, because He gave everything. Only you know where that fine line is between effort and trusting.

Now, let's wrestle a bit. You know this is what He wants. Suppose you are considering doing something that, if let go, may resolve itself. But left alone, it could get a lot worse. It's one of those harder 'right' versus easier 'wrong' kind of deals that is really somewhat minor, but nevertheless will impact your character. If you give in and refuse to stop, and consider, ponder, think, and even pray about what you are about to do, then you have already let it go too far. Sure, you can do what you have always done and just plow ahead, but in doing so you miss worlds of opportunity – for good. However, you must be the one to draw the line on when enough is enough, because only you can fully know when letting it go comes from your faith in His work and not a belief in your own. You also are the only one who can tell when you are "resting" in Him vs. just being lazy. A warning: "A little sleep, a little slumber, a little folding of the hands to rest — and poverty will come on you like a thief and scarcity like an armed man. (Proverbs 24:33-34) Make no mistake: every day is a battle to find that balance. Are you winning that battle? Sometimes winning means – like Jacob – just holding on, to Him!

"Blessed are the poor in spirit, for theirs is the kingdom of heaven. Blessed are those who mourn, for they will be comforted. Blessed are the meek, for they will inherit the earth." (Matthew 5:3-5)

Versus

"Blessed is the one who does not walk in step with the wicked or stand in the way that sinners take or sit in the company of mockers, but whose delight is in the law of the Lord, and who meditates on his law day and night. That person is like a tree planted by streams of water, which yields its fruit in season and whose leaf does not wither— whatever they do prospers." (Psalm 1:1-3)

Chapter 3

FOR RICHER FOR POORER

P rosperity vs. poverty. So, who is blessed, the prosperous or the poor? Which is it? Are the prosperous really evil? Do I really have to be poor to be spiritually mature? Why this vagary in scripture? The question belies the problem. For one man, he is way too hung up on money. Leaving that man to struggle could bring him closer in his relationship to God – or he could waste his life in pursuit of the 'almighty dollar.' For another man, money has no hold on him. Either in great prosperity or in relative poverty, he gives sacrificially and is not swayed by having much or having little. And his neighbors are watching. Prospering him may save many souls. The fantastic truth of God's words is in their simplicity and complexity at the same time. Psalm 37:4 says,

"Take delight in the LORD; And He will give you the desires of your heart." Seems pretty straightforward, doesn't it? Get pumped about Jesus, and He'll give you the things you want – the desires of your heart?

If you know Him, then you know there is a bit more to "taking delight in the LORD." The casual reader says, "Where is my stuff? I'm pumped! I'm excited about Jesus. So now I should get good stuff!" In much of scripture, the unspoken meaning behind the words is really the main point of the passage. The Hebrew teachers or rabbis employed a discussion technique when studying the scriptures, called a "remez."

> Remez demonstrated a deeper understanding of the scriptures and was employed as a kind of verbal marshal art when the rabbi would engage his students or other teachers. It is one of the methods that Jesus used quite often when He quoted scripture. Using this method, the teacher quotes a verse from the Bible, but the point he is making is from the verses surrounding the one he quoted.[6]

The verses surrounding Psalm 37:4, or its context, are addressing a complete trust and commitment to the LORD. The condition of receiving the desires of your heart is to delight yourself in the LORD. A heart that delights in the Lord probably doesn't desire a bunch of stuff.

The point is that as I delight in Him and begin to think and act more like Him, I begin to desire the same things that He desires. And if you know Jesus, you know He really isn't too caught up with stuff! The prosperity promised in Psalms (35:27, 37:4, 84:11-12) comes on the heels of a transformed heart that couldn't care less about stuff and cares more about people. Not only does it sound unseemly to go around claiming that Jesus wants you to have lots of things – especially if you are hung up on things – but, it is just a lie and therefore evil for anyone to teach you that! What He is after, more than anything, is anything that brings you closer to Him.

So, on the other hand, if you are "poor," could you actually be the 'blessed'?

In the summer of 2006, our entire family went to Nicaragua to serve with a missionary family that was located there. They had established a flourishing ministry – in the Managua, Nicaragua dump! An entire community, hundreds of adults and children, made the Managua dump their home. Mike, the missionary with whom we were working, had established a school – procured a building, teachers, furniture, and support – inside the dump. Over a hundred children filed into that school every day, and the meal they served at noon was usually the only meal those kids got any given day.

I struggled with this for some time, wrestling with the necessity of going outside of the country to serve the poor. Don't we have our fair share of poor right here in our own country? Well yes, but the fact is there are few or no options for most of those folks who do not find themselves in a country as wealthy as the U.S., with shelters, warming/cooling/feeding centers and a plethora of government programs to provide aid for them. Whatever the motivation, be it pity or a desire to fulfill God's call to care for the poor (Proverbs 29:7, 31:8, 9), missions are extremely eye-opening and instructive. We go on those trips expecting to minister to those people, and in a clever twist, the tables are turned and we are brought face-to-face with our own abject need for a daily dependence on His provision.

The truth is, people in those seemingly dire circumstances have less standing between them and God than we do. They wrestle every day for their own survival. Yet if you spend any time with them at all and get to know them, they are some of the most un-stressed, thankful, generous, and peaceful folks you would ever know. We go to these places and to these people who have nothing. We come from where we have everything and go to where they have 'nothing' – or so we think! We bring some of our stuff in hopes of helping stem the tide and the effect of their relative poverty, but we know that we are only putting a temporary "finger in the dike". What we really hope is to have a platform from which to address people with whom we otherwise would never have the opportunity to talk. We hope to show them our Master. We hope to show them Jesus.

No matter how dire the situation, most folks are exceedingly grateful, thankful, and happy for our help. But they are also far more content in their circumstances than I could ever imagine. The danger I am in, living here in relative comfort, is beginning to think that my world is *the* world. When we are actually the anomaly and the other 780 million people in the world who cannot go to a sink and turn on clean, running water are the norm. And maybe even *because* of all our creature comforts, they should be sending missionaries *here* instead of the other way around! In God's economy, we live in an upside down world. More is less. Less is more. So you tell me who are the rich and who are truly poor.

Don't get me wrong! On balance, there really is nothing wrong with wealth. But nothing (especially in this country) will test the heart more severely than having it, losing it, and being asked to share it. Seems like, if peace is what you seek, then getting rid of some money might be your best answer. I have known people on either end of the spectrum. I know wildly wealthy people who are amazing people of faith. They give away over 50 percent of their income and live well below their means. I also know wildly wealthy people who are actually very good at making money, but spend everything they've got on themselves. Both appear somewhat content, but the latter are clearly on edge. Both are daily being tested. Both have their hearts laid bare to any casual observer of their lives. One is mastering his resources and passing the test of his heart. The other is being mastered by his resources, and the stress shows.

We can possess so much and still have nothing. Isn't it obvious that being wealthy is an intensely difficult and subtle test? It's almost – well no, it definitely *is* – a trap. Jesus Himself marveled at a young, wealthy guy once. Jesus offered the guy the opportunity of more than a lifetime, an opportunity for all time! Jesus offered him a chance to join His posse – to be one of His disciples. Everyone for all of eternity would have known that dude's name! One of the disciples! Are you kidding me!? Of course it didn't end well for any of them, but no one knew that at that point! St. Peter, St. Paul, St. John, St. Rich Dude... It was right there in his grasp. And as the young (rich) man walked away from the Creator of all living things, Jesus takes a long breath, lets out a heavy sigh and says, "Again I say to you, it is easier for a camel to go through the eye of a needle, than for a rich man to enter the kingdom of God." (Matthew 19:23-24)

Jesus taught more about money than He taught about Heaven and Hell – combined! Do you think maybe He knew how hung up on it we would be? It is so hard to maintain a proper perspective on money, but the fact that we get so defensive and even emotional when we are questioned about it should give us pause! With constant sober judgment, I have to keep my motivation in check and wrestle not only with what He teaches, but with my own tendency to elevate money to an 'end' and not a 'means.' That is, I make it my tool and not the thing I am building.

"Believers who are poor have something to boast about, for God has honored them. And those who are rich should boast that God has

humbled them. They will fade away like a little flower in the field." (James 1:9-10 NLT)

Finally, how do you know how much is enough and where to draw the line, and what to give away and what to keep? That is between you and our Creator, my friend. And I'm pretty sure that on this one, you are going to have to wrestle!

"...And he will be called Wonderful Counselor, Mighty God, Everlasting Father, Prince of Peace!" (Isaiah 9:6)

"Peace I leave with you; my peace I give you. I do not give to you as the world gives. Do not let your hearts be troubled and do not be afraid." (John 14:27)

Versus

"Do not suppose that I have come to bring peace to the earth. I did not come to bring peace, but a sword." (Matthew 10:34)

Chapter 4

WAR AND PEACE

S o which is it, Peace or No Peace? If Jesus came to finally settle things between God and us, why does He say things like what we read in Matthew 10? This sounds like a total reversal of Isaiah 9, and John 14! Our expectation of this "good God" and His Son who came to "make all things new" is that things will be, well, better. This contradiction seems unfair – at least without considering how completely messed up the world is (or will be) at the point of His return. This argument carries with it the full weight of the greater question of *evil* that sparks the question for so many: "…if there is a God and if He is so good then why is there so much evil in the world?" The deeper question in such an inquiry is in fact the existence of God in the first place. It is interesting that the person asking this question has no problem identifying and acknowledging that there is such a thing as evil. But for evil to exist, someone has to make a moral judgment about what is evil. Are any of us going to be that judge for everyone else? And to conclude there is no God, they likewise first must believe themselves so enlightened as to assert that they have come to the end of all human knowledge and understanding of the cosmos; that they have determined there is nothing more than what they, themselves, have observed, experienced, or come to know. To know this, though, they would either have to know everything—in which case they would *be* God and thus refute their own claim that they do not exist—or admit that they are just regular people who are too proud to admit that they don't know everything and maybe, just maybe, there is something more in that small percentage of all knowledge that they haven't mastered yet! Welcome to the family of believers!

Sorry. It is just so disingenuous to rail against evil and knowingly gripe about its prevalence, all the while discounting the pink elephant in the room—that for there to **be** good, the opportunity for evil must also exist, and someone has to make a moral judgment, someone who knows everything! To get hung up on the existence of the principle of good and evil is just a ruse, a distraction, a weaker point that is just one more obstacle to throw out before addressing what is really gnawing at us: "Is He really there or isn't He?" Jesus tells the disciples in one setting–as He is about to leave them–that He leaves them with "peace," and in another setting, not long before that, when He is sending them out to go tell people what they had seen, He flatly states that He did "not come to bring peace... but a sword." And He doesn't stop there! He goes on to tell them about "Brother betraying brother to death," and being "... hated by everyone because of me...." I contend that these apparent contradictions are purposeful and meaningful!

In John, He is speaking to all of them for possibly the last time before the cross. He knows the literal hell that is about to break out in Jerusalem in the morning, and yet, He says something like, "Peace I leave with you...." But He continues, "Not as the world gives peace." Without getting ridiculous about the Hebrew and Greek translation of the word "peace" in John and Matthew–because they both mean the same thing in this case–anyone who looks honestly, with a true desire to understand and not just win an argument, can look at scripture within its context and gather what God is getting at! Again, He says, "Not as the world gives peace," in John. Shouldn't this tip us off to what He really intends, or at least that He is driving at something different than what it appears? Because to most of us–let's be honest–peace is the total absence of any type of struggle. It's *easy* street!

The "world" thinks of peace as a state of zero conflict. And that is not what He is saying here. In fact, what He is getting at is a sense of easiness in the face of certain pain or struggle. "Not as the world gives peace," pushes past normal expectations for stress and anxiety in dire or difficult situations. You have seen examples of this. Terry Sedlacek walked into a church on a Sunday morning in 2009 and suddenly opened fire on Pastor Fred Winters with a .45 caliber pistol, killing him. A week later, Fred's wife Cindy went on national television and spoke freely and openly of the pain she was feeling over her and her daughters' loss. She went on to speak of her concern for Terry Sedlacek, her husband's killer! She said that she and her daughters (ages eleven and fifteen) continued to pray for Terry, that he would come to know and accept their forgiveness and that of Jesus Christ through the ordeal! The lady had just lost her husband a week earlier. Now, you might say she was still in shock and hadn't effectively dealt with her loss yet, but when the court dates came months later and the guy was deemed too crazy to stand trial, Cindy repeated her calls for prayer for the killer.

We hear stories like this all the time. Scott and Janet Willis lost six children when their van exploded on the freeway in Chicago in November of 1994, and the media clamored to see how these people of faith would respond when it was found that the accident had involved a driver who obtained his license illegally through fraud. The Willises spoke of their faith that they will see their kids again one day, and of forgiveness that kept their hearts from darkening. In horrific circumstances, unimaginably, they found peace!

Though we hear the stories, we stand at a distance and question if we could do likewise and continue to live without becoming bitterly angry. For the believer, there is hope! Ponder for a minute the alternative. If you are out there and you do not ascribe to a faith and belief in something *more,* what are you left with? The only alternative when tough times or tough circumstances come – and come they will – is despair. All you are left with is despair.... In fact, Jesus does say that we *will* have trouble. (John 16:33) It is coming like death and taxes (fortunately, He addresses both). "But," He continues, "take heart, because I have overcome the world." The "Peace I leave with you" in

John speaks of a confident hope *in the face of trouble* and not a sure protection from it.

By the time I turned sixteen, got a license, had a few jobs and started to make some money, I began to contemplate how and what I was going to do with the rest of my life, you know, out from under the dictates of my parents – on my own. I am not sure when this comes for most folks, but observing my parents wrestling with things like bills and taxes and all the things that owning and running a household involved, it kind of freaked me out! How on earth was I going to learn all that stuff and get it all straight? It was the specter of responsibility closing in on me. In the midst of that, I found great comfort and solace in the fact that I did not have to have it all figured out – yet! Fortunately, I reasoned, there were people and powers who had a greater understanding of such matters (Mom and Dad). And they would work all of that out for me until such a time as it became necessary for me to learn. Then there would be people on hand to teach me what I needed to know – teachers , instructors, professors, and the U.S. Army, in my case. I could rest in the fact that these "powers" had my best interests in mind and would handle all of those details for my benefit!

That is the "peace" Jesus offers. Faith is like that. Look, I know the cultural elite and the "enlightened" may call this fanciful, la la land, unrealistic, and child-like thinking. But what do these "enlightened" know of true love, living for something more than yourself, and a peaceful calm in the face of death? Like several folks I know who are fighting cancer right now, that peace is no psychological coping skill, it is a gift, and a glimpse of something – more! It is why – as they say – there are few atheists in foxholes. It's true! The only thing that really keeps us from losing it in situations like that is an understanding – you know that you know that you know – that this is NOT all there is. This is NOT the end. It's really just the beginning!

Without that confidence and conviction, I don't understand how folks otherwise function – aside from bravado, which gets plenty of people killed I suppose! You could get all dark about it and just say to yourself, "Well, this is the end for me, so I guess I'll just go out guns blazing." But good luck staving off the terror of becoming worm dirt for eternity or the thought of the sum total of your existence fading into someone's distant memory. The deepening passion and unexplainable peace that grows in my heart, and in the hearts of countless people of faith who daily face death in cancer wards, battlefields, missions, inner cities, and in foreign prisons of decidedly anti-Christian states, simply cannot be explained as some kind of misplaced ignorant and blissful hope. First of all, their stories are too numerous and compelling. Secondly, they are consistent in that we have been hearing their stories of peacefulness and faith in the face of death from the time of Daniel in the lion's den, around 500BC, to Pastor Saeed Abedini who is currently being tortured in an Iranian prison. Abedini was sentenced on January 27 of *2012* to serve eight years in the notorious Evin Prison after he was accused of running a network of Christian house churches in Iran. Abedini knows that he may never walk out of that place. People will simply not die for a lie, or exhibit peaceful resolve over a simple hope that the fairytale is true. There is something more! And we know it! Abedini definitely knows it!

"For God did not send his Son into the world to condemn the world, but to save the world through him. " (John 3:17)

I understand the "save the world" part. But what about that sword in Matthew 10? Could saving the world necessarily involve swinging a sword? What happened to the warm cozy "Prince of Peace" Christmas story about the "Wonderful Counselor"? (Isaiah 9:6) Well, think about that for just a minute.

If, as we have been saying, we see the culture disintegrating all around us, and becoming more and more evil and debased, wouldn't it make sense then that someone who is kind of teaching against the "things of the world" would likely be opposed to the world – or what it has become? To save the world, these warring factions of God and culture are going to have to come to some kind of settlement. In settling a dispute, some heads may need to be cracked! I'm guessing that's what the sword is for!

Christ ultimately came to earth to bring peace (Luke 2:14; Eph 2:14-17) but when people choose to follow Jesus, they will often face division and conflict, even within their own house-holds. To choose loyalty to family over loyalty to Christ even disqualifies a person from being one of His disciples. (Luke 14:25-27)[7]

We know the battle for our souls is raging all around us. Our enemy has so infiltrated our media that he is almost undetectable in his subtlety. Truly, our television programming really is not what it used to be. A couple weeks ago I was looking for a movie to watch with my eleven and sixteen-year-old sons that would be appropriate for all of our collective ages. So I pulled up a review of a movie that looked pretty safe on a reputable Christian movie review site. Hey, I don't need my boys learning profane vocabulary inside the sanctuary of my own home. I know they hear that garbage enough outside my doors, I don't need, nor do I want to reinforce it in my home!

So, anyway, I'm looking at this site and they pretty much have the whole film dissected nicely into these categories that take you completely away from the enamor of the title, plot, or cast and kind of sterilize the content into a 'just-the-facts' manner that effectively gives you the 30,000-foot aerial view of the film. Here are the categories that they post for each movie: Positive Elements, Spiritual Content, Sexual Content, Violent Content, Crude or Profane Language, Drug and Alcohol Content, Other Negative Elements. After wrestling to find something that wasn't ridiculously juvenile – sorry, but I'm just tired of all the talking, flying, soccer, basketball, and base-ball-playing dog movies – I finally settled on something that looked, um, safe. As I began reading the review, I was stunned! Even a seemingly innocuous, silly, cop-turned-ghost-who-avenges-wrongful-death movie contained some highly offensive material when broken down in this manner. And even though the film was low in sexual content, decent in its moral messaging, off the charts – in a bad way –with (slapstick) violence, and had some considerable alcohol use, what struck me the hardest, and really killed the whole thing for me, were these words under the heading **Crude or Profane Language**, *"Jesus' name is abused at least a half-dozen times, and God's is misused once or twice."* Let that sink in for just a moment. This TANKED the movie for me!

Shocked, I went back and started looking at other movies I had seen that I thought were actually decent, moral, movies. It would blow your mind how many times, in what look to be relatively innocent movies, you find "Jesus' name is **abused**...". You may think me prudish to get so hung up on a common expression that people really don't mean to be offensive. But listen to this, *"**Jesus' name is abused.**"* The image that those words conjure up in my head is of the beating administered to Jesus pretty much the entirety of the film "The Passion of the Christ". I guess seeing it put in that way, *"abused"*, just brought home to me how ridiculously casual I had become about such things. An innocent "OMG" here, the tolerance of a "Jesus Christ, that's a big gator" there, and suddenly we have slipped so far into the profane that we don't even flinch when children start throwing around words you hardly even knew when you were younger. And we wonder how our programming has slipped so far so fast. Hmm.

Which leads to another question: Why are movies that are okay for you not okay for your kids? Or reverse that: Why are movies that are not okay for your kids somehow okay for you? Whatever negative influence you would readily shelter your children from is equally as damaging to you! Isn't it?

The carnage of the battle for our affections is on display daily. It happens more often in private, but publicly, we see the cycle repeat itself year after year like the broken record of the AGES. How many professional athletes, CEOs, and industry execs who make their millions and then wind up in jail, bankrupt, or dead, does it take to see that it is all a lie? How many actors or musicians who have some level of success then wind up in rehab, in court, or with a needle in their arm, do we have to have to watch crash and burn to get the message that fame and fortune will never satisfy? No, the peace that Isaiah was talking about, the peace that the angels told the shepherds about at Christmas, and the peace that Jesus gives to the disciples before He leaves in John 14, is between His Dad and us – not us and the world! There is a vast difference! We know this, yet we still feel somehow cheated when difficult times or circumstances befall us! He even says we will definitely have trouble in the world. (John 16:33) But the peace He offers to the disciples, and to us, is between us and God, NOT us and our employer, our government, our friends, our spouse, etc. Which would you rather have? Think for a moment before you answer that question.

Truthfully, I do not get how anybody manages to muddle through this life without some sort of hope outside of what they can manage for themselves. These trials that are common to all of us—you'll notice that Christians are not exempt—would be debilitating without the hope that somehow, some way, we will get through them; the hope that no matter the outcome, we are never alone; the hope that there really is someone bigger in control; and the hope that there is a sure and certain reward waiting!

Remember Jacob? He was God's chosen vessel to bring about the nation of Israel, but he had to go through some serious stuff, not to mention a dislocated hip, first. And it never really got any easier for Jacob. God is not going to let us skate through, either. Crazy to think of the trials as blessings in themselves, but what God offers is not safe passage, but a hand to steady us as we walk through stuff that will most certainly test us, and in some cases push us to our limit.

"I'll never leave you or forsake you" doesn't mean two cars in the garage and no bills! It means "I will go through it with you."

Remember all the old Sunday school stories? Noah and the Ark, Abraham in the desert, Joseph in Egypt, Moses in the desert, and on and on.... Almost every story is an odyssey of hardship and being brought through some serious, often life-threatening junk! The only guy who doesn't really have it too hard is David's son, Solomon, but read the book of Kings in the Bible and see what happened to him!? Seven hundred wives, good grief!! Think about that. From Adam to Jesus to John marooned on an island, the consistent theme is of one hardship after another. Could it be that we are at our best – or the best is extracted from us – when we are in the crucible, being pushed, tested beyond our comfort zone and beyond our understanding? We just live such sheltered and comfortable lives now that it seems even a day without electricity is a bummer and a major trial eliciting a prayer request! Ha!

Tell Paul about your electricity problems. Here's a guy who was struck mute by lightning (sort of), flogged, beaten , had multiple attempts on his life, had to escape from city to city because of angry mobs, stoned three times, left for dead, thrown into jail several times, shipwrecked, left in the open sea overnight, bitten by a viper, and finally imprisoned again in Rome at the end of it all. And this is the guy who opens most of his letters talking about how thankful he is! How did we get it so backwards, then? How have we become so bent on creature comforts and relative ease of life as an indication of how "blessed" we are? By all indications, a better gauge for how blessed we are might be how much trouble we are experiencing! I'm just saying!

So with that perspective in mind, maybe peace is the sword! Maybe difficulty and trouble are the gift. Maybe the worse things get, the better our chances are of getting closer to Him and experiencing a real and lasting peace. Think of the guys He was talking to when Jesus said, "Peace I leave with you." (John 14:27) Do you know what happened to ALL of those dudes!? All but one were killed in some really nasty ways!!![8] The one guy who wasn't killed was boiled in oil, then poisoned, and when that didn't work, he was marooned on an island and placed in isolation! Regardless, it was a hard road for all who were His disciples, so why do we expect it to be any different for those of us who now call ourselves His followers? Here is one thought: the more hosed we are, the more messed up things get, the more trouble we get into, the more we tend to lean in on Him. Don't we!?

When our most lofty, eloquent prayers become, "Oh, God please help me!" it is then that we finally reach the point of complete dependence. Pride is gone. All striving and control is lost. This is God territory. How many times have you heard the story of otherwise God-less people who, when they find themselves in dire circumstances, say things like, "God, I haven't talked to you in a long time…" or, "God, if you are really there, if you could just get me through this…" When we have nowhere else to turn and have come completely to the end of ourselves and finally relinquish control, THAT is the point He steps in. So, if it is "blessings" we seek, breaking us down to the point of finally turning wholeheartedly to Him may just be the answer, for some. With "fear and trembling" I have purposed to keep myself in a constant state of abject need because of this principle!

Okay, I'm exaggerating a little, but a healthy dose of humility (delivered often times via my own children) and a frequent falling on my face before Him have kept me in check and possibly staved off circumstances that would otherwise have brought me low. But if "low" is what I need, "low" is what I'll be! Do I really think God is "cause and effect" in that way? Do I honestly believe that my actions or humility can change how God acts or responds in any given situation? Some rail against such thinking, as a kind of threat on God's sovereignty. What was it He said? *"...if my people, who are called by my name, will humble themselves and pray and seek my face and turn from their wicked ways,, then I will hear from heaven, and I will forgive their sin and will heal their land"* (2 Chronicles 7:14). If you will do this, then I will do that. He says it, A LOT: Exodus 19:5, Genesis 4:7, Deuteronomy 4:25-26, Deuteronomy 6:25, Psalms 91:9-10, Isaiah 1:18-19, Matthew 6:14-15, Matthew 21:22, Romans 8:31, 1 Corinthians 16:22, 2 Corinthians 5:17, Revelation 22:18-19! It's all through the Bible! My love and affection for my kids is absolutely unconditional – no if/then's. BUT, man, there are absolutely consequences for everything that they do or leave undone.

We get so far out on the limb arguing over how God acts or doesn't act, and we totally forget that He is a father and so close to us in that role. You can bet there are going to be consequences when my youngest son nearly burns down the house and barn, playing with the embers of a fire in our burn pit. It will be a while before the little bugger gets to play his video games! And he won't be doing several other things he likes to do for a while either, until I cool off. Those are consequences. But he is still my son, and in spite of the consequences (and my frustration) he will still join us on family outings, maybe a movie, and his place at the dinner table is never in question. And I reminded him that I still love him when I tucked him into bed that night. I do everything I can to put his mind at ease that we are still okay. But I do not remove the consequences.

Of course there is a cause and effect relationship between the peace we all seek and our obedience. But even when we screw up and He busts out the paddle, if our heart is broken by what we've done, and not defiant or proud, then He meets us in the midst of the ugly consequences. Somehow there is peace in the midst of even punishment.

He said that He is close to the brokenhearted and saves those who are crushed in spirit. (Psalm 34:18) So I'm thinking, better to be in front of Him, near to Him, talking to Him *before* things get ugly. Look, I know that is still no guarantee and even genuine humility may not ward off trouble in life. But the fact is, when trouble comes, if I have been regularly in conversation with Him – which usually calls for a bit of humility – nothing seems all that horrific. Wouldn't it be awesome to be unshakable, content, bulletproof!? "Dad, I wrecked the car – Okay, honey, are you all right?" "Darin, we have to let you go – Oh, well, okay." "Darin, I'm really sorry, but it's cancer – Wow, really, well, okay. What's next?" And if you don't think that last example is possible, I know a few people I would like you to meet.

No, we are not superhuman, but unshakable, maybe! "Peace," He said, "not as the world gives peace…", "…peace, which exceeds anything we can understand." (John 14:27 paraphrased; Phillipians 4:7 NLT)

It is in the struggle that we actually find the answers we seek. It is in the wrestling and contending for His blessing that we experience Him. But we find blessings in the strangest places! If you have ever been on the mission field (everyone needs to have one trip on their bucket list), then you understand this principle. Spend some time with folks who live in dire circumstances, yet somehow still display such unimaginable joy – if you want some perspective on blessings.

*"Dear brothers and sisters, when **troubles** come your way, consider it an opportunity for great **joy**. For you know that when your faith is tested, your endurance has a chance to grow. So let it grow, for when your endurance is fully developed, you will be perfect and complete, needing nothing"…bulletproof!* (James 1:2-4 Darin K. Jones Version (DKJV)) :)

Wouldn't it be nice not to stress about – money, tomorrow, stuff?

"Not only so, but we also glory in our suffer-ings, because we know that suffering produces perseverance; perseverance, character; and character, hope." (Romans 5:3-4)

Okay, I know this sounds like emotional boot camp, but isn't what we face daily a war on our emotions? Sure, I can grit my teeth and grunt and strain and try to gut out everything that life may throw at me, but sooner or later I will come to the end of myself. And at that point, when I enter the crossroads, I will have a choice to make: hope or despair. In his book When God Doesn't Make Sense, James Dobson writes,

When I was a boy, I heard a mystery program on radio that captured my imagination. It told the story of a man who was condemned to solitary confinement in a pitch-black cell. The only thing he had to occupy his mind was a marble, which he threw repeatedly against the walls. He spent his hours listening to the marble as it bounced and rolled around the room. Then he would grope in the darkness until he found his precious toy.

One day, the prisoner threw his marble upward – but it failed to come down. Only silence echoed through the darkness. He was deeply disturbed by the "evaporation" of the marble and his inability to explain its disappearance. Finally he went berserk, pulled out all his hair, and died.

When the prison officials came to remove his body, a guard noticed something caught in a huge spider's web in the upper corner of the room.

That's strange, he thought. I wonder how a marble got up there.

As the story of the frantic prisoner illustrates, human perception sometimes poses questions the mind is incapable of answering. But valid answers always exist. For those of us who are followers of Jesus Christ, it just makes good sense not to depend too heavily on **our** ability to make the pieces fit – especially when we're trying to figure out the Almighty![9]

Faith isn't blind. Hope is not just for children at Christmas time. Having the humility to consider that you simply do not know everything, and the belief that there is someone bigger, smarter, and more powerful than you, who really does have things under control, turns off the stress and the need to try to control everything. Knowing that He is working it all out, in spite of how it looks, gives me great peace. The "enlightened" may see this as naïve or even juvenile, but a hope in only what you can grasp sooner or later comes to an end. As oversimplified as that may seem, I know in my bones that it is true. I don't want to understand God completely! That would mean I had come to the end of Him. I prefer knowing that He is beyond my comprehension and His resources and ability are unlimited. It doesn't mean that I don't contend with Him for an understanding of what or WHY I have to go through something. After all, it is in that contention that I begin to understand. I can drive myself crazy with the "why, why, why did You do this to me" fitful plea that really isn't looking for an answer, but an outlet for my frustration. Or, I can grab onto Him – in anger, yes, possibly, but also in earnestness – and we can wrestle. In my forty-nine years of experience, He hasn't flinched once.

"For we know that our old self was crucified with him so that the body of sin might be done away with, that we should no longer be slaves to sin—because anyone who has died has been freed from sin." (Romans 6:6-7)

Versus

"So the trouble is not with the law, for it is spiritual and good. The trouble is with me, for I am all too human, a slave to sin." (Romans 7:14 NLT).

Chapter 5

SLAVE OR FREE

L ike many of us, Paul gets a little tongue-tied trying
to articulate the "profound mysteries" of God from
time to time. Later, he goes into a rant about wanting
to do good but not doing it and the not doing of it
but the sin in doing it is what... Wait, now even I'm
confused.

Anyway, we get the idea that even Paul has
some issues with sin. So are we slaves or aren't we?
Because, hey, if Paul is struggling with it, let alone
struggling to define it, how am I ever supposed to do
much better? If, as he says in Romans 6:7, we are free
from sin, then, hey, stop sinning – just stop it.

Good luck with that.

Okay, the obvious things like murder, stealing,
lying, adultery, and worshiping idols—those things

are easy enough to stop. But how about not hating on someone; fudging a little on an expense report or your taxes; lying about what time you got up; looking at another woman (or man) with lust in your heart; spending every spare moment either on work or on Facebook (like that is not idol worship); or mindlessly surfing the Internet? Not so cut and dried, is it? So, since we all struggle with something, how could anyone hold me to some higher standard than everyone else? By asking this, are we trying to imply that the things we clearly recognize as bad (or sin) are really sort of okay since everyone else struggles with them also? Because that would be some pretty bad reasoning.

But this is how many of us attempt to justify ourselves. We absolutely know something is wrong, and yet our minds go into "spin" mode immediately, in an attempt stop feeling any guilt about that admittedly bad thing we just did, or are thinking about doing! "Well," we think, "at least I am not as bad as that guy over there!" Even in our relationship with God Himself, we begin to weigh our standing with Him against those around us instead of against the one single standard by which (or whom) we are truly measured. Because we all know where we would stack up. He became a man so He could see what all the *not sinning* hubbub was about! He is the standard, not "that guy over there". And against *that* standard, I'm afraid it would not be pretty!

Do you really think it was any easier for Him than it is for any of us? Sure we'd like to think, "Well, He was God, so of course it was easier for Him to resist than it would be for us." True, yes, He is God, but He was also fully human! "Therefore, it was necessary for him to be made in every respect like us, his brothers and sisters, so that he could be our merciful and faithful High Priest before God. Then he could offer a sacrifice that would take away the sins of the people." (Hebrews 2:17 NLT)

So before we try to go too easy on ourselves because we are not God, understand this: There is nothing we have faced or will ever face that is any more difficult than what He faced while here on this Earth. Also, there is no temptation we face that He hasn't faced – and overcome! Yet, He tells us, "No one is righteous – not even one" (Romans 3:10 NLT) and "But you are to be perfect, even as your Father in heaven is perfect." (Matthew 5:48 NLT) He expects us to be holy! "But we cannot *not* sin," you say. I get it. None of us is without sin, nor will we ever be. But instead of flying off the handle in the other direction (sinning so that grace may increase – Romans 6:1), and doing just what we think is good enough or better "than that guy over there," we have to do a gut check!

What is behind my weak justification? Why am I struggling to give my best to this? If I strive for perfection, I will never make it! Remember, He said to cease striving. And we already talked about works not getting me there! Besides, we are under grace! All are familiar arguments and all true. Nevertheless, all are excuses – some that I have used – for just being too lazy to overcome my desire to remain in the place that I am. To not grow, not fight the culture, not say and do what is right, good, true, and pure, is just wrong. And our hearts know this! Like Jacob, we come to that moment – a defining moment – when we have to ask ourselves, "Do I really believe this stuff? And is it really going to make a difference in my life if I put forth the effort to do the right thing?" In our hearts and in our heads, the battle is on! It is gut (heart) check time! I suppose the pressure Jacob felt, given his situation was a matter of life or death, may have been a bit more motivating for him. But what is it going to take to get some of us to get off our dime and simply do the right thing?

Honestly, do you ever wonder this? Some people are just so completely hard-headed, it boggles the mind! We hear the story of the CEO, or government agency official, who embezzles several hundred thousand dollars from their organization, or the teacher or pastor who has an illicit affair, and we wonder, "Is the right thing really that hard to do?" We have come so far in terms of image management and settled so deeply into our comfort zone, that to change course and actually do the more difficult, right thing takes extreme pressure or circumstances. This gives "stubborn pride" a whole new meaning. Maybe we are not so unlike Jacob. It might just take our issue – whatever it is that holds us back – becoming a matter of life and death before we finally wake up and at long last grab on to God so hard and so fast that it would take Him dislocating a hip to get us to let go!

So, again, are we free, or still slaves to sin? "Don't you realize that you become the slave of whatever you choose to obey? *(There is that pesky "choosing" thing again…)* You can be a slave to sin, which leads to death, or you can choose to obey God, which leads to righteous living." (Romans 6:16 NLT) I think the point is, this is going to be an ongoing battle. As believers and followers of Jesus, we understand His death has set us free. And yet, resisting sin is still such a struggle. That leads us back to Jacob. We were made for that struggle. Let's not fool ourselves, God knew Adam was going to blow it! And now we have to struggle. We are supposed to struggle. The struggle strips away all the image management and reveals who we really are. The struggle exposes our character. It exposes our hearts.

The U.S. Army Ranger School understands this! Strip away the bottom, most basic layers of Maslow's Hierarchy of needs (like food, shelter, and sleep), and who we are inside comes to the surface pretty quick! In the first week of this course, those basics are significantly called into question, and your mind begins to reel. These types of schools are designed to expose the character of the individual soldier, and to weed out the weak. On the first day, standing in formation, the instructors tell you to look to your right and then to your left at the two individuals standing next to you. Then they tell you that one, and possibly both, of those individuals will not make it to graduation – and they are right! These schools are difficult. They are a constant struggle. Their purpose is not only to train soldiers for operations in difficult environments, but to expose the heart, mind and character of the individual. You cannot stand idly by and let the course go on around you. Freeloaders who think they can just blend in and coast through drop out early on! You have to engage and you have to wrestle.

We are tested daily. Every opportunity, every difficulty, every word choice, every decision is our own kind of challenge. Will we take the "road less traveled" and choose the harder right versus the easier wrong? Will we try to straddle the fence with a half-hearted attempt to avoid gossip or complaining? Will we turn our backs and run from temptation? Or will we go soft, feeling that the good I've done will surely outweigh the bad and so allowing a little self-indulgence will be okay? I work with cardiac doctors – surgeons. I hear stories all the time of patients who come in for major heart surgery. Usually it's the young (-ish, forty-five to fifty-five-year-old) executives I hear about. A guy comes in for a double bypass of two clogged arteries on the heart. The doc performs a very cool bypass procedure and sews a new section of artery in where the old, clogged section was. Effectively, the doc has saved the guy's …life!

Doc and the cardiac team of physicians give the guy some strict dietary guidelines for maintaining his new life with the new plumbing. You can just guess what happens next. Most go right back to the same lifestyle and same messed up diet that landed them in surgery. They justify that, well, now they have new, fresh arteries that have no disease, so it would take them another forty-five years to mess that one up, and by then, they really wouldn't care! They had been given a new life, a new chance, and the freedom to do what they want and not die. And what do they do with that freedom? A few get it! They stick militantly to the recommendations of the doctors and dieticians. But like I said, most blow it!

We are free. But unless we continue to work at it, our stupid sin nature will come right back and slap us in the face. Craziest thing in the world, if you ask me, to ever become complacent about the hard fought freedom that Jesus won for me. Sitting back on His laurels (as it were) and expecting that since I have proclaimed my belief in Him, I will never be tempted or persuaded or enticed to do things that I know I shouldn't, is just naïve. Holding on to what is right and good takes effort. Get this, though: I am not suggesting that we need to be doing things to earn His favor (see Chapter 2). Nor am I suggesting that we somehow try to repay Him, because we just cannot – any more than we can stop doing dumb things like judging others, wanting their stuff, putting things ahead of people, and generally not loving others as much as ourselves .

Although those seem like small things, they reveal something. You guessed it! They reveal our heart! Funny how it is the small seemingly insignificant things that "out" us. Judging someone to be a fool versus sticking a knife in them doesn't seem like a big deal, but the heart behind both is equally dark! So, walking the line between being fully aware of our tendency toward selfishness, or evil, yet not shackling ourselves with guilt and self-loathing is the point! That's what it means to be "freed from sin" yet a "slave to sin." Can both be true at the same time? Can God be a man? Ask Jacob!

"God created mankind in his own image…"
(Genesis 1:27)

Versus

"By our very nature we were subject to
God's anger…" (Ephesians 2:3 NLT)

Chapter 6

TO SIN OR NOT TO SIN

So maybe this is not a real big hang-up for most. You can't really argue the sin nature deal when the most adorable, innocent, spotless, and untainted one-year old will go toxic on you if you take their binky away! Being made in the "image and likeness" of God may be news to some. That's right, we were made in the image and likeness of God! And, as I read in Genesis and begin to get a little puffed up about my potential greatness, having been made in the "image and likeness" of God (don't you just love the sound of that), I start hearing that all-too-familiar, overly self-affirming voice in my head! ME! Yes, I'm pretty awesome. But then things turn dark pretty quickly in Genesis. It takes no time at all, really, for Adam to blow it – on so many levels!

Yeah guys, I hear you all screaming, "Whoa, wait one minute–IT WAS EVE who bit that apple first, then she gave it to Adam and dragged him into her deal!" So many great lessons have come out of this story of our humble beginnings. I have heard some muse, "Maybe Adam would have been better off without the help-mate who got him busted." Another speaker observes, "He was standing right there when the whole thing went down, and said nothing, but took and followed her lead without uttering a word!" You may say that the serpent approached her because he knew that she was the weaker of the two (1 Peter 3:7). Okay, okay, but ultimately who did God come looking for when He knew that they had blown it? I find it very telling that when God comes to confront them for what just happened–because of course He knows everything already, and the question is really a set-up–He comes looking for Adam!

This is the first instance of the Maker of the universe saying to us, "Guys, you have got to own up to your responsibilities." It doesn't really matter if you believe in an egalitarian society or gender-neutral responsibilities in life. God is going to hold YOU (fellas) responsible for what goes on in your house, in your family, and in your relationships. This is the message that we all struggle with, starting usually around junior high and continuing on for the rest of our lives – you are responsible! Pull up your big boy pants and own it! The good news is, you are also able, because we all were made in His image.

The major religious thinkers (except for Irenaeus and Tertullian)[10] all pretty much agree on what was meant by "image" and "likeness" in Genesis 1:27. They define image/likeness as nonphysical characteristics, rational ability to reason, logic, morality and character. So then, using this definition of "likeness," Genesis is saying that we are like God in our rational thought and character – if, that is, we are not tainted by something like, oh, sin!

What a peculiar word, *sin*. There is almost a universal understanding of what sin is. Yet, here in the 21st century, the word is so laden with cultural dogma that it has taken on almost a whole new meaning. Sin has been transformed from a completely wrong, dark, visceral evil, into some kind of universally accepted shortcoming that, since we all do it, shouldn't be judged. And anyone who utters the word is seen as judgmental and labeled a hypocrite! We think we have become so enlightened, when really all that we are doing is justifying ourselves. As any addict counselor would tell you, we would do well to step back and first acknowledge our addiction! We are broke! But I digress....

It would be simpler to imagine that in His supernatural form, God looks like people, with arms, legs, etc. But the great spiritual thinkers of the day say "no," we don't look like Him, but we have the potential to think like Him! Wow! How could I have literal God-like potential and still be so completely messed up? To have the potential for greatness, there must be an equal opportunity for failure, or greatness wouldn't be all that great. If there were no opportunity for failure, none of us would be any better than, well, average. It's kind of like the question of evil. How can such a good, kind, and loving God allow so much evil in the world? If we agree that God is the embodiment of love (go back and read the foreword) then for Him, or massive amounts of love, to be possible there must be an equal possibility for horrific evil, since evil is the exact opposite, or absence of love.

At every moment of every day of our lives, we make choices – light shirt, dark shirt; cereal or eggs; pass the car or wait for your exit; take the call or let it go to voicemail; get up early or sleep five more minutes. You get the idea. Not every decision is that critical but there is typically a good and a better decision, and sometimes a good and a bad decision. By the way, it should be very telling about our nature – ever since the incident with the apple – that the better way is nine times out of ten perceived to be the more difficult way. We tend toward those things that we know will lead to our destruction – sugar, gossip, less exercise, bad movies, bad books, bad web sites. Even the Second Law of Thermodynamics (the law of entropy) agrees that the universe is moving toward disorder, not order. Things are running downhill, not improving. And unless we alter the course or maintain it somehow, something is going to break. We have to work at life. We have to decide. In other words, all of life is like running up the down escalator! If you stop working or decide not to decide and just go with the status quo, you have made a decision, and you are headed down!

This is just one more way that we see the story of the garden working its way out in our world now. Both (Adam and you) possess such beauty and unbelievable potential, and yet in other ways, both can be so dark and completely, well, evil. But dark as our actions, nature or tendencies may be, they do not supersede or somehow override our potential for greatness. That potential resides in all of us. We are ALL made in His image – He says so! So those daily choices we make have an impact on the forming and shaping of our character: daily, moment by moment.

Every good decision strengthens our ability to follow up with another good decision, and another. Every bad decision drags us further down, and our character begins to degrade–rot, that is. Those simple, daily decisions are what determine our greatness. Man, I want to be great! Don't you?

Which brings us again to what is in our hearts–selfishness or greatness! We can't have both. Because, here is the hard, fast, truth, and the secret of greatness: "...whoever wants to become great among you must be your servant." (Matthew 20:26) Herein lies what many see as the chief dichotomy of God! Greatness–equals–servanthood.

Greatness is Servanthood

Greatness is the measure of our ability to put ourselves aside and "do" for others. It is the counter-cultural stumbling block that our world just can't wrap its head around. "The message of the cross is foolish to those who are headed for destruction!" (1Corinthians 1:18). It is the principal example that Jesus gives us of corporate and individual leadership. Want to be an extremely successful and effective leader? Serve those under you! It is the anti-worldly, stop everything, playing field-leveling, secret power, "check mate" move of all time! If you have ever had a rival, or someone you have been contending with, suddenly turn and do something nice for you—not a patronizing compliment or gesture, but a genuine act of servant-hood—then you know the overcoming power of this principle. Another way to look at it might be that the inner drive that you are sensing for greater accomplishment and greater "self-fulfillment" may actually be the call to pour yourself out for something or someone *else*!

I have this distinct and growing feeling that the rat race of my life has kept in check my only shot at greatness. The vision and the drive for my life's goal and purpose seems held just beyond arm's reach by nagging menial tasks, like earning a living.... The tyranny of the urgent has managed to keep this truth at bay for many years! It is this single inexplicable *truth*: I am missing out on something! Something in us calls out—no, screams, "You were made for MORE!" But the MORE that we get into our minds is not necessarily the MORE that He intends for us. His is better! Our MORE would be the fame and/or fortune or just comfort that we selfishly seek. Creature comforts that, once obtained, still somehow do not manage to fill the void and allow us to *rest*, assured that THIS was what we had been seeking all along! Material or financial gain nefariously leads us further away from the

"MORE" that would so fill our hearts and so thrill our minds that we would shake our heads in disbelief and remorse at having taken so long to get to it! You were built – that is, given a very specific skill set developed by enduring some very specific life experiences – to serve others in a very specific way.

Yeah, yeah, I know, that doesn't sound like a rocking, awesome, adventurous mission for your life. The serving thing just kills it for most, but why!? Because it is not ME-centered! How on earth have we become so narcissistic? We have allowed Hollywood and a counterfeit-truth culture to shape our idea of what adventure and excitement really are! The impact your life has on someone you help, someone you sacrifice for, expecting and taking nothing in return, will endure possibly for generations! And it will leave a mark that may well alter the future of many! By contrast, let's say you clock the world record time in the mile. A few track enthusiasts may know your name, and you may get into a couple record books (until someone else comes along and bests your time), but your record would have served only you. And your influence would be limited to possibly inspiring someone to seek your record. Nothing more!

Did you know that there once existed a single man who, more than a century ago, made one move... that still dramatically affects how you live today? He was a thirty-four year old school teacher, but on the hot, humid day of July 2, 1863, Joshua Lawrence Chamberlain was in the fight of his life. [And he forever changed ours!] *A former professor of rhetoric from Bowdoin College in Maine, he was now a Colonel in the Union Army. Chamberlain stood at the far left edge of a group of eighty thousand men strung out in a line across fields and hills, stretching all the way to a little town called Gettysburg, Pennsylvania. Earlier that day, a Colonel Vincent had placed Chamberlain and his men of the 20th Maine at the end of that line, saying, 'Whatever you do, you can't let them come through here.' If the Confederate Army overran them, the rebels would gain the high ground, and the Union Army would be quickly defeated. In essence, eighty thousand men would be caught from behind on a downhill charge with no protection. To win, the grey clad Confederates would have to come through Chamberlain.*

As the story goes, after the fifth charge on the hill by the rebels and a fifth costly stand by the 20th Maine, the men were out of bullets, seriously lacking any kind of energy, and out of men to hold off one more charge. But when it came, Chamberlain, faced with the choice of doing nothing or doing something, chose to act. At the sixth charge, Chamberlain, lacking any resources, ordered his unit to 'fix bayonets' and made a counter charge down the hill. This stunned the enemy, who retreated, many of them leaving their loaded weapons on the hill.

Historians have determined that had Chamberlain not charged in that one moment, the rebels would have won Gettysburg. Further, historians tell us, had the rebels won at Gettysburg, the South would have won the war… today we would exist as two countries… we would live on a territorially fragmented continent much like Europe – North America would be divided into nine to thirteen countries. Which means: When Hitler swept across Europe in the 1940s, had Chamberlain not charged on that afternoon so long ago, there would not have existed a United States of America to stand in the breach. When

Hirohito systematically invaded the islands
of the South Pacific, there would not have been
a country big enough, strong enough, wealthy
enough, and populous enough to fight and
win two wars on two fronts at the same time.
The United States of America exists as it does
today because of a single man: One thirty-
four-year-old schoolteacher and one move he
made more than a century ago.[11]

This is called "The Ripple Effect" or in the case
of Andy Andrews' book, quoted here, the "Butterfly
Effect." Small acts of servanthood, done almost unno-
ticeably, cause ripples that may affect all of us for
all time!

Lonzo Green, a semi-successful country music
artist, was visiting relatives in Tennessee in the
summer of 1950. His nephew, Jimmy, had bragged
around school about his uncle who was staying with
them right there in the apartment on Lauderdale
Court! Jimmy had befriended a dark-haired boy from
the "wrong part of town" who had his own guitar
but didn't even know how to tune it, much less play
anything on it. So Jimmy invited his friend over after
school to meet Uncle Lonzo. Jimmy's parents however, made it clear that the dark-haired boy was not

invited to come inside the house. Folks from that part of town were known as "white trash," and under no circumstances were they to come into Jimmy's house.

Lonzo had agreed to meet the boy out on the curb and help him tune the guitar. When the shy, soft-spoken boy arrived at the end of the lane, Lonzo popped out the door to go and meet him. "Then he noticed that the boy's guitar, obviously inexpensive, doubtless secondhand, was tethered by a piece of string." He tuned the battered instrument and before he would allow the obviously self-conscious boy to leave, "Lonzo played and sang a familiar hill country ballad, then another and another. Shortly the haunting reticence in the boy's eyes was gone, replaced by the joy of the music. After Lonzo had taught the boy to play a few chords on the guitar, the youngster thanked him again and was on his way. He was not invited inside. Not then. Lonzo Green would never meet him again." However, Lonzo would later consider the encounter and wonder at this single small act of kindness and its affect on the young dark-haired boy – Elvis Presley.[12]

Chamberlain did not get credit for winning the Civil War. Lonzo is not credited with inspiring Elvis Presley. But, as we now know, their influence in acting right-ly, good-ly, and putting others ahead of themselves – becoming, as it seems, a servant — changed *everything!* Hundreds of stories like these have been written and still more could be told that demonstrate the far-ranging effects of simple acts of kindness. We are moved by the effect of people placing other's needs above their own. People who do this are seen as heroic! Although we give acclaim and celebrity status to TV, film, and sports stars, there is something inherently different when we see someone sacrifice for someone else. Soldiers, police and firemen and women, servants! Why do these acts of sacrifice touch a nerve so much stronger than our fascination with celebrity? Acts of sacrifice strike at something deeper, a simple truth that is hard-wired into our DNA: though we have this annoying tendency toward being selfish, self-seeking, and self-preserving (there's Jacob again), we (each and every one of us) do hold the potential for self-sacrificing greatness! It is what you were made for and you know it! But given the duality – or dichotomy – of our sin-ridden, yet God-like image, for us to realize our potential, we are going to have to wrestle!

"In him we were also chosen, having been predestined according to the plan of him who works out everything in conformity with the purpose of his will" (Ephesians 1:11)

Versus

"But if serving the Lord seems undesirable to you, then choose for yourselves this day whom you will serve..." (Joshua 24:15)

Chapter 7

BEGGARS CAN'T BE CHOOSERS

So, do we choose God, or does He choose us? Are we predestined, preprogrammed, and without a say-so in the matter? Or are there some things God can't force or predetermine? Election vs. Free Choice, the Armenianism vs. Calvinism debate! This is the struggle between those who hold to the freedom of people to not choose to follow God vs. God's sovereignty and His choosing some and not others.

You probably cannot even believe that I would have the audacity to take on such a long-standing, deep-rooted and intellectual argument. Such far-ranging arguments should be left up to scholars and theologians, you are thinking! This argument, and apparent contradiction between certain scriptures, has caused church splits, small group arguments, family feuds, quarrels, contention, frustrations, and many a seminary student's all-nighters pouring over scripture and commentary on scripture to gain a foothold. Why? This is not exactly one of those watershed issues that trouble the hearts of the common man or woman. But it is a point of contention for those who honestly wrestle with the idea that we humans act only under the direction of a God who loves, yet also holds the controls. Does He order acts of kindness as well as acts of great evil? If He is in control, then how does He allow such great evil to persist? If He is not in complete control, then He is not really sovereign. The difficulty here is for those of us who operate within the confines of time as a linear function (stay with me) to wrap our brains around the fact that we are in relationship with a God who operates outside of the confines of time.... He invented it. Chew on that for – a while!

So, right now, God sees Jesus on the cross – as if it were happening right now. Right now, God sees our next President being elected. He sees forward and backward – as it were – in time, because He is not confined by time. So He knows, or foreknew, every choice that you will make, because He sees it! This does not negate your choosing, and He may allow some difficulties or hardships in your path to get your attention or incite a decision on your part. But still, I believe, the choosing is left to you – inside the confines of His will. I know that sounds like a cop-out, but I cannot fathom a circumstance or a scripture that limits God. However, He did exercise immense restraint in limiting Himself to take on the human body of Jesus! So He may choose to limit His own influence. Does that clear it all up for you?

The other problem occurs in our most basic understanding of what power and influence even is! We tend to think and expect power to express itself in the ability to command respect and impose our will. We trip over the greatest dichotomy of all that God's perfect power is expressed most absolutely and clearly in His sacrifice – of His own Son! It's that "upside down world"; power in weakness; first are actually last, and last will be first; grace to the humble, condemnation to the proud; meek inherit everything! So if His expression of power was to sacrifice His son, imagine how backwards our understanding of His expression of His love for us might be, much less our understanding of who chose whom! Okay, let's step back for a minute and consider what a hard-line stance on one side or the other of the predestination fence means. It amazes me that folks will go completely "hard core" with either the notion that we have no choice but instead are created for salvation – or condemnation. Or, equally ridiculous on the other hand, is the idea that God is so detached that He just started the ball rolling and stepped back to watch, and the rest is all up to us.

First, let's not think more highly of ourselves than we ought! The rabbis who studied the scriptures inside and out, backwards and forwards – well enough to argue their points in remezes – and dissected every "jot and tittle" of scripture, still somehow missed the Messiah in His coming, His appearing, His public ministry, and His death, all of which were clearly foretold in that same scripture. So what makes us, who may have done some reading and study of scripture, though certainly not the level of study of a rabbi, think that we have such a clear understanding of how He chooses, and how He will return? If *they* doubted then, and continue to doubt now whether Jesus could really be the One, then it is the height of arrogance for those of us who spend less time reading the scripture than we do eating, doing housework, or watching college football (ouch) to say that we have the scriptures definitively figured out! I'm not proposing a form of relativism or personal interpretations. There are objective verities, absolutes, and irrefutable truths that are not up for argument! But the fact that God has left us to struggle with some things (pre-trib vs. post trib; once saved vs. losing salvation; immaterial God vs. material provision; Calvinism vs. Arminianism) must give us pause when we start heading down the road of saying "Thus Saith The Lord"!

In Philippians 2, Paul says, "...continue to work out your salvation with fear and trembling...". In Romans 8, he says, "And those he predestined, he also called..." In Hebrews 6 (NASB) it says, "In the case of those who have once been enlightened...and then have fallen away." Ephesians 1 says, "For he chose us in him before the foundation of the world..." Revelation 3 (NASB) says, "Behold, I stand at the door and knock. If anyone hears my voice and opens the door, I will come in to him..." And on and on it goes. Face it. There are strong arguments, backed by scripture on both sides of this fence! And we may argue the context and intent of the original writers all day long!

But, I will contend that the truth on this one is somewhere in the middle. Problem is, we have to exert our own bent, our own opinion, on the argument. Let me explain: our messed up human nature will take hold of either of these arguments and even without our realizing it, will express our bias in the way we live our lives. This is my own, simple observation.

The firm believer in our predestined inclusion into God's kingdom tends to be less interested in personal evangelism in the form of loving their neighbor. Even though their intent may be to reach out in obedience, love is not the principal driver. Because if their neighbor is "**in,**" well hey, there is really nothing they can say or do to affect that. What's done is done and what happens *happens* – according to His will. So I can go on about my day with no real concern. Because after all, if God wills it, it will be done... whatever "it" is!

This, to me, lacks passion. It seems devoid of urgency, drive, emotion, love. Say I brought my wife flowers and she was just blown away by the gesture, and she asked me, "Why did you do this?" If I were to say to her, "Well, I am doing what I'm supposed to do," do you think she would even want those flowers?[13] We are reduced to pre-programmed – yes – robots. In the case of the staunch adherent of our free will, a limited God leaves all kinds of room for concern, worry, questioning, and doubt concerning our standing with Him. It causes a subconscious drive to please God with our actions and the things we do for Him or in His name. God is sovereign. I believe that with every ounce of my being. He is in control. I trust in that, and it gives me confidence. But God is also LOVE!

And no matter how you try to define it, it is impossible to have love outside of risk, outside of choosing. If something is mandated, it just ain't love! If it is ordained, predisposed, predetermined, or in any other way manipulated, by definition it is not love. And God is LOVE. (1 John 4:8) As *Newsweek*'s John Meachem says, "Love coerced is no love at all, only tyranny, and God wanted us to choose whether to love him or not, to obey him or not."[14]

So then, is it useless to even have the arguments if we are not going to ultimately reach some conclusion? Not at all! The argument is what it is all about, really. The argument is what drives us to dig deeper and try to figure it out – to continue the quest! The argument is what gnaws at us to figure out what is right and what it really means to me! Oh, sure, we want a conclusion. More than that, we want to be right! We want to win the argument! But then what? We walk away, smug and self-important. That kind of pridefulness has been around for a LONG time.

So let's step back into the argument for a moment. As unfathomable as it would seem for someone to actually have an intimate relationship with the God of Heaven's armies and then somehow walk away, it is equally as unfathomable to think of being in His court, in fact to be His second in command, His archangel, and still choose to walk away! But Lucifer did. Was Lucifer once saved? He was as close to God as any being besides Jesus has ever been. According to 2 Peter 2:4, a number of the angels of Heaven actually sinned, resulting in their being cast down with Lucifer. The fact that an angel could sin means they must have had a choice, a free will. They made a choice to disobey God. They were not limited in their knowledge and awareness of the bigger picture because they were living in Heaven outside the limits of linear time! They knew the ramifications and something – I believe pride – still drove them to side with Lucifer.

As crazy as that sounds, don't we do much the same thing when we claim to have the definitive answer on a matter in which scripture has left room for argument one way or another? That is the danger of our "thus saith the Lord" proclamation. It so easily and subtly slides into pride. Does it diminish God's greatness that there are some spiritual matters that He may have left up for discussion, argument, or even wrestling? We want the answers, and that is a *good* thing because it drives us to search, ask, dig to know Him more. On the other hand, our prideful nature wants answers also. For what? Closure? So that we can move on – past God!? Guess what? He's not going to give us some of those answers. He doesn't want us to move on. And in those instances when we argue, fuss, and fight about what may seem unanswerable, there is actually a third alternative. Even in the case of choice vs. predestination, there is a third possibility that for me has become my default: faith. Not blind faith – accepting faith!

What I mean is this: take the facts as far as you possibly can, and at that point accept the possibility that you do not have the complete answer. You hold to where the facts lead, leaving room in your heart for something more to be revealed. Because ... "Now we see things imperfectly, like puzzling reflections in a mirror, but then we will see everything with perfect clarity. All that I know now is partial and incomplete, but then I will know everything completely, just as God now knows me completely!" (1 Corinthians 13:12 NLT) Faith is NOT just accepting things as they are and throwing up your hands. Faith is having the humility to accept that you just do not know everything!

Nowhere in life has this principle, this concept, this universal truth come more clear to me than in my relationship with my siblings. Funny how these deep truths tend to show themselves so clearly in relationships – can you say Jacob!? Man, as a younger brother, I GET this! And now as the father of an older brother, it is a particularly hot button for me. You older siblings out there are just going to have to take this with a grain of salt because of the obvious baggage I carry as a younger brother, but the fact is, YOU DO NOT KNOW EVERYTHING! Honestly, I wonder if all of the conflicts in life wouldn't be significantly reduced if man could wrap his brain around this single defining principle that goes back to, oh, third grade. To accept this, yes, there is a fair amount of "letting go" that we must somehow do! And that just takes faith.

So I accept, on faith, that He really does have our best interests in mind. But I don't stop there! I don't just roll over and say, "Que sera sera...!" (If you were born after 1970, you may have to look that one up) I take Him at His word and make a daily practice of checking my arguments, and my opinions against the truths that I find in those words. Because, the amazing thing about those words, if you are honest when you read them, is that they are unabashedly, and painstakingly true in what they say about me. When you read them with any kind of serious intent to see for yourself if they are true about you, and "test the spirits" that wrote them, you will inevitably find yourself uttering the same faint, deep, "uh hmm" under your breath that I do! And if I am serious about having a relationship, I talk with Him–throughout the day as challenges and victories come, and ask the difficult questions of Him, "What on earth did You mean by THAT...?" Or, "Why did it have to happen that way?" That's called prayer! And I believe He just can't get enough of it! So if this is where the argument brings us, humbly, before Him, then the argument, the tussle, the wrestling, has accomplished what I believe to be its primary purpose!

So, did we choose Him or did He choose us? Do you *really* want the answer to that question? Ask Him! He can clear that up for you!

"Do not judge others, and you will not be judged." (Matthew 7:1 NLT)

"Therefore you are inexcusable, O man, whoever you are who judge, for in whatever you judge another you condemn yourself; for you who judge practice the same things. (Romans 2:1 NKJV)

Versus

"Speak up and judge fairly; defend the rights of the poor and needy." (Proverbs 31:9)

"Look beneath the surface so you can judge correctly." (John 7:24 NLT)

"If your brother or sister sins, go and point out their fault, just between the two of you. If they listen to you, you have won them over." (Matthew 18:15)

"Those who continue in sin, rebuke in the presence of all, so that the rest also will be fearful of sinning." (1 Timothy 5:20 NASB)

"If people are causing divisions among you, give a first and second warning. After that, have nothing more to do with them." (Titus 3:10-11 NLT)

"We urge you, brethren, admonish the unruly, encourage the fainthearted, help the weak, be patient with everyone." (1 Thessalonians 5:14 NASB)

"Take special note of anyone who does not obey our instruction in this letter. Do not associate with them, in order that they may feel ashamed." (2 Thessalonians 3:14 NIV)

Chapter 8

DON'T JUDGE ME!

Here is the rest of Matthew 7 in context:

"Do not judge others, and you will not be judged. For you will be treated as you treat others. The standard you use in judging is the standard by which you will be judged.

And why worry about a speck in your friend's eye when you have a log in your own? How can you think of saying to your friend, 'Let me help you get rid of that speck in your eye,' when you can't see past the log in your own eye? Hypocrite! First get rid of the log in your own eye; then you will see well enough to deal with the speck in your friend's eye."(NLT)

T hat headliner, the Matthew 7:1 verse, has become the most quoted Bible verse in the United States, surpassing John 3:16 on the fly. "Don't judge me," or "Don't judge," is almost a mantra now! These words are usually uttered when we have done, or are about to do something that we know we should not be doing! So much so that what we really ought to be saying is, "Okay, so I'm going to go ahead and do this thing that I pretty much know I really shouldn't be doing, but I don't want you to tell me it's bad – even though I know it is!!!" Or even simpler, "Hey, I want to be bad and I don't want you to call me out on it." Sure, I know that is not the heart behind every use of that phrase. But sometimes we have to take a step back and take an honest look at what we are saying and doing and judge ourselves for ourselves. I think that is called discipline!

I know, I know, that's a dirty word – discipline. But how or why do we not expect our lives to be a total train wreck if we refuse to exercise even a modest amount of it? Besides that, we need each other, really, to keep from going off the rails. Isn't it usually the folks who think they've got life wired, who are accountable to no one, that end up in the biggest messes? So my buddy, my friend, my brother corrects me – consistently. If he/she only ever strokes me, it is of no use to me. Once I have been able to take that log out of my own eye, it is then worthwhile and helpful – not to mention much better received – to help my friend remove his. Do you see it? At some point, even though we are admonished here not to judge *hypocritically*, we are at some point – once we have removed the log from our own eye – going to deal with the speck in our friend's eye! The real lynch pin is the motivation behind our actions, or (again) the heart that is behind the correction. Heard that somewhere before? If, by pointing out where a friend has stumbled, you are intending to help restore that friend to a solid (or reconciled) relationship with the Lord, then it's all good! If, on the other hand, your motivation is simply to point out the other person's wrong – which really means you are just trying to elevate yourself – then obviously your heart is in the wrong place and you are just as (if not more) in the wrong as your stumbling friend.

Somehow, we have gotten lazy about stopping the flow of our thoughts from our minds to our mouths. The only good thing about that is, unfiltered, our thoughts actually reveal our hearts. The problem is the delicate balance in knowing what should be called out, and just shooting off at the mouth! Sometimes, something needs to be said! My concern is the notion that we have gotten so sloppy about "valuing others above yourselves" when we do so! (Philippians 2:3)

Hypocrisy is the bane of Christianity, if not the whole world! Who doesn't despise being manipulated, or being lied to because somebody has some hidden agenda? Talk about making my blood boil! The younger brother in me rages to the surface at times like this—feeling mistreated, told something just to get me to do something else or to react! THAT is how I became a *fairness* fanatic. And fairness is cool, as long as it doesn't slide over into just wanting to make sure that guy over there doesn't have more stuff than me! There, again, is the tension between what is right (fairness, goodness, honesty), and what can almost undetectably slide over that fine line into pride and selfishness because someone got more than me. I cannot control their intent—I have to let go of that and allow God to deal with them! But I certainly can control my own intent.

You see the struggle? I have to fight to keep my motives pure; to NOT be a hypocrite. THEN I will see clearly to remove the speck out of my brother's eye. My point is, hey, let's not throw judging completely under the bus (after all, there is an entire book in the Bible devoted to the people God appointed—to judge!), but let it be tempered with sober awareness of my own faults and with a heart (motivation) to help build up and not tear down. Can we all agree that some things are just wrong? I believe that everyone on the earth *does* have a sense of what is right! Harming, hurting, or torturing kittens (and children) is just evil, right? I mean, everyone agrees! Helping the poor, widows, and orphans is good, right? Wait, haven't I heard that somewhere!? "Open your mouth, judge righteously, and plead the cause of the poor and needy…" and puppy dogs and little orphaned kids. (Proverbs 31:9, DKJV) "Learn to do right; seek justice. Defend the oppressed. Take up the cause of the fatherless; plead the case of the widow." (Isaiah 1:17) Don't we all agree that is good? I mean, COME ON, basic right and wrong is in every one of us.

The only way we differ on this is how often we give rise to that "still small voice" inside calling for us to DO THE RIGHT THING!!! Every time we ignore that voice and go on doing just what we want to do, it becomes more and more faint. We become numb or insulated from it. But trust me, listen to it. IT will save your life! Listen! And the voice gets louder. Listen! Because, It is Him.

Sometimes God just needs to put skin on. If I had not encountered Him in the form of some significant people in my life at critical junctures, I shudder to think about where I would be at this moment.

In 1998, I was working for a start-up medical device company that was designing a new device for the retrieval of kidney stones. That year (or around that time) I attended a major urological conference in New Orleans with my company. One of the doctors I called on was helping to develop this device, and he was attending the conference. We had arranged earlier to have dinner with him and his staff, who were accompanying him at the conference. This particular doctor was quite (internationally) well known in his specialty and had drawn the attention of several device companies, all of whom were vying for some of his time while at the conference. When the officers from my company and I approached him to ask his preference for the dinner, he said that he had numerous offers for dinner, and that – since our company was the "cool" company – he would rather just go for drinks afterward with us. Asked what venue he preferred, he said, "I don't know, we'll figure that out later."

Because of our numbers, we rented our hotel's minibus and went to pick the doctor up at his hotel. Once he and his team climbed aboard the bus, he hollered out, "Okay, where are we going?" Several people rattled off the names of a number of different nightclubs and bars in New Orleans, where we could go. "Cheeta's it is!" came his reply. "Cheeta's. Hmm," I thought. Sounds like an interesting – uh, club. Is that a – yep! It's a strip club.

Interestingly, it was around that same time that I had begun to develop a strong relationship with a guy in my church with whom I played pick-up basketball a couple days per week. Tony was a landscaper, and he was/is a little rough around the edges. He doesn't mince words, if you know what I mean. Tony calls 'em like he sees 'em, and doesn't use real flowery speech to do so. He is also what you would call a genuine "man of God." Tony and I and a couple other businessmen would meet every Wednesday morning at 5:30AM at his shop to pray, and occasionally he'd mix up an awesome potato, vegetable, and garlic breakfast that I still salivate over when I think about it. We'd check in, fill each other in a little on how things were going, talk about any issues that we were dealing with, then we'd pray for around thirty minutes–sometimes more–and be on our way. None of us really had the time or patience for useless banter, so we'd pretty much cut straight to the core of anything we were wrestling with, or concerns that were on our minds. At 5:30 in the morning, surface level conversation is just annoying to anyone! We challenged one another regarding what we said versus what we really meant or were thinking. These were some of the most challenging, and yet life-giving conversations that I have ever had. The difference was, I absolutely knew the motivation behind every difficult word they spoke was one of concern and a true desire to help me improve.

Anyway, back to New Orleans. So I claimed to have this belief and this life and lifestyle of a follower of Jesus Christ. Yet here I was about to walk into a strip club in New Orleans. Some of my colleagues who were there with me knew me, and knew where I stood. And I suppose their eyes were likely all the more curious about how I would handle this. The bus pulled up to the club and I sat there wrestling with the right thing to do. The doctor, my doctor, from my account, would surely be offended if one of his entourage (particularly his local representative) refused to go in, thereby indicting him and his obvious sin. I could lose the account, estrange the doc, make the leadership from my company look foolish, lose my job, you name it! I had to think fast, because the bus was emptying into the entrance and I would soon be the only one left. A couple of my colleagues said, "Come on, Darin, let's roll!" In the pressure cooker of those few seconds, my mind reeled and kicked straight into self-preservation/justification mode! "Well, if I just don't face the stage and carry on a conversation with the doc or some of the people on his staff, then it's not unlike going to just any bar. Jesus ate with tax collectors and sinners, right? I'll avert my eyes – yeah, that'll work. Some of the medical residents in his entourage are women, I could strike up a conversation with them and sort of negate the fact that I'm in a **strip club**. One of the residents is a Buddhist. I will have a spiritual conversation with her about religion and profess my faith and that will cover everything." This last thought was actually the plan I ran with as, yes, I crumbled in the face of the enemy and went into Cheeta's.

Was there a voice in my head screaming at me to STOP, and not go in there? Well, yeah, of course He was. But there were also the others telling me my job was on the line, among other things. And in my pathetic weakness and fear, I listened to the latter.[15] I caught a cab back to our hotel with a couple of the other guys who left a little earlier than the others, claiming we had to be back at the booth for the conference early in the morning. Once back at the hotel, I simply could not shake off the nasty, dark, drippy, slimy cloak that seemed to be hanging on my shoulders. I took a shower – nothing, still there. Dang!

"Okay, I'm calling Tony, he gets me, he knows I'm just a struggling guy with a few weaknesses. I'll confess to him and it will be all good. Yeah!"

So it was just before midnight, and I called Tony on his cell. I figured he knew something was up when he saw me calling at that time of the night, so as soon as he picked up and said, "Uh-oh, what's up?" I laid it all out there for him. His response was something like this: "Wow, Bro, that really sucks. I won't say that I haven't been there because I have and I'm really sorry. So now what are you going to do?"

I told him, "What do you mean, 'What am I going to do?' I've already done it. I told you!" He said, "That's cool, Darin, but I am not the one you offended." I snapped back, "Well, I already feel like scum and I've asked God for His forgiveness and admitted it to you, but look, I can't tell Beth, she will never understand!"

As long as I live, I will never forget his next words. They have been some of the most instructive, meaningful, and loving words I have ever been told. He said, "Well God and I have already forgiven you. But you have got to tell Beth, or I will." He gave me one week from the time I returned home, so I told her the night I got back just to make sure he didn't beat me to it.

Sometimes we need people to judge us! Sometimes we need to feel the sting of conviction in being judged, righteously. Especially if we've been "found wanting"!(feigned reference to Daniel 5:27) We live in that tension between wanting to help someone become better, and tearing someone down so that WE can feel or look better. The difference is vast, and wrestling with the warning to "judge not" balanced with the charge to "judge righteously" will unquestionably expose the true motivations of our hearts.

Lastly, there are more than a few other places where the Bible actually does have a bit more to say about judging:

- Be not deceived (Matthew 24:4, Luke 21:8, 2 Thessalonians 2:3, Eph 5:6, Colossians 2:8) requires judgment.
- Test the spirits (John 4:1)–to test requires judgment at some level.
- Jesus congratulated the church at Ephesus for rooting out false apostles (Revelation 2:1-3). This required some form of judging that what they were teaching was wrong.

Some like to point out that Jesus often met with and ate with "sinners and tax collectors" as a demonstration that He never called these people out on their

sin, so we should likewise keep our judgments to ourselves. This is true, we hear Him say that He didn't
come for those who "say, 'We [can] see.'" (John 9:14
NASB), but He came to "seek and save the lost."
(Luke 19:10) There is, however, an important distinction between the people He was addressing. In
the case of Matthew (before Jesus offered him a new
'job'), the people at the party at his house were people
who made no claim to be people of God or His followers. But when He is addressing the scribes and
Pharisees and sometimes the church-going folk in the
temple – those who claim to be enlightened, who say
"We see" (John 9:41 NASB), His conversation with
them was quite different! (check out Matthew 12:34!)

Funny how we are all for it when Jesus **blasts** the
religious people, "You snakes! You brood of vipers!
How will you escape being condemned to hell?!"
BAM!!! (Matthew 23:33 emphasis added...) But we
get all defensive when the bright light of truth, spoken
to us by someone other than Jesus, exposes a flaw or
weakness. On one hand, we do not want to be called
out, especially by someone who we decide has WAY
more flaws than us. On the other hand, if what they
are saying is true, is it possible that their "calling me
out" was actually an attempt to help me keep from
screwing up, and not an ill-intended "pot shot" made

to bring me down? We avoid the tension of judging or being judged righteously. When the thing that needs to be said is true, or when the criticism about you is on target, it strikes a nerve. It hurts. It's tough. But could it be that living in that tension is actually the sweet spot that will allow you to reach higher heights and become the person that you were intended to be? The struggle to love and not go soft, judge but not from pride, and serve but not yourself, is His command and our challenge. We do need the occasional gut check to ensure that our motivation is in the right place. That is where that bad word (discipline) and some really honest, close, good friends come in. Something about iron rubbing up against iron comes to mind... (Proverbs 27:17) Again, our motivation is exposed – when we wrestle!

"But anyone who does not love does not know God, for God is love." (1 John 4:8 NLT)

Versus

"They will throw them into the blazing furnace, where there will be weeping and gnashing of teeth." (Matthew 13:42)

Chapter 9

LOVE AND HELL

Pretty harsh sounding, isn't it? A lot of people really struggle with even the idea of Hell. They wrestle with the idea of a God who claims to be the embodiment of love actually condemning one of His children to a place that is referred to as a "place of torment." But who said or made the law that everything about God had to make us feel warm and fuzzy? Why couldn't He design a place of "eternal torment" made for those who never wanted to have anything to do with Him? I'm not saying that was His intent. In fact, I believe that everything that is nasty, cruel, dark, evil, gruesome, lonely, wrong, and bad, is just wherever He is absent! If He's not there or not in it, then *nasty* is what you are going to get! What is more unloving: allowing someone who never wants anything to do with you to never be with you; or creating someone for the purpose of never being with you? Who is to say what that "eternal torment" will be? Okay, we can pretty much assume that it won't be too good. People who are gnashing their teeth are not having a really good time. But giving those folks the exact thing that they have been demanding all their lives, namely distance from Him, isn't cruel, it's just.

See, we don't get to *not* play the game by the rules and then expect that no matter how we play, we still get to win and go on playing. Like so many of the principles of God, I have found that the understanding and perspective of a third grader clears it all up! "Everything I really needed to know about God, I learned by the third grade!" Maybe that's why He said that we had to become like a child to enter the Kingdom of Heaven! (Matthew 18:3) The third grader understands that if he doesn't share his toys with the other kids in the sand box, pretty soon nobody is going to play with him, and he will be all alone in the box. He may think that is cool at first, but once there, completely isolated and alone, while the other kids run and laugh and play together, he will long for some interaction, for some friends. And there will be none!

I don't see demonstrated anywhere in scripture a big "slam-dunk" on Judgment Day. Like the perfect gentleman that He is, God ultimately gives us what we asked for all our lives. For some, this will mean an entree into His presence, His kingdom, a place referred to as "Paradise"! For others it will simply be distance from Him. No "hammer" falling, no trap door, just exactly what they have been asking for all along. As for the "blazing furnace" and "weeping and gnashing of teeth," well, given that at that point we will be more spiritual than physical beings, I'm thinking that at least a good portion of that torment is massive regret–which could be worse than the flames! Ever seen someone gnash their teeth when they found out that they were very close on an important test question, but still got it wrong? Ever seen a kicker miss a game-saving goal or field goal? They gnash their teeth, grinding out words something like, "Dang, I wish I had a do over!" I'm guessing there will be a lot of that kind of gnashing! Either way, it's going to be a raging, perpetual bummer!

Is it difficult to reconcile a loving God with a punishing God? After all, Hell and the devil are His creations. They are His Hell, and His devil. But doesn't it stand to reason that if He has such a large capacity to love, unless we are all preprogrammed, then there must be an equally large opportunity for great evil. Likewise, as dark as the human spirit can get–and

Hollywood does a pretty good job of depicting the depth and breadth of our depravity—there is equally as intense an opportunity for towering, blazing, infinite light, and good, in us! The latter only comes by keeping the dark side in check. It is necessary and good to acknowledge, and with a measure of self-awareness, deal with our own brokenness without trying to justify ourselves. But, there is an extremely fine line between acknowledging how messed up I really am, and not continually flogging myself to prove or exact proper humility.

In the 13th century, a group of Roman Catholics, known as the "Flagellants", took on the practice of whipping themselves to demonstrate their religious fervency. Dwelling on the wrath of God can produce much the same attitude. Paul engaged in this wrestling match and demonstrated pretty aptly his best attempt to walk this fine line:

"I have discovered this principle of life—that when I want to do what is right, I inevitably do what is wrong. I love God's law with all my heart. But there is another power within me that is at war with my mind. This power makes me a slave to the sin that is still within me. Oh, what a miserable person I am! Who

will free me from this life that is dominated by sin and death? Thank God! The answer is in Jesus Christ our Lord. So you see how it is: In my mind I really want to obey God's law, but because of my sinful nature I am a slave to sin." (Romans 7:21-25 NLT)

Slave to sin, yes, but I am also a "Child of the One True King," and no longer defined by the wreckage behind me, but instead constantly "...press on to possess that perfection for which Christ Jesus first possessed me." (Philippians 3:12 NLT) He would have never asked us to follow Him without giving us the ability to not sin – so stop it!! Oh, and do not give me that "nobody can be perfect" excuse – that's not what I'm saying! You know what I'm getting at – yea that, stop it!

As I see it, He doesn't cast anyone into Hell – we choose to go there. Didn't He create those two options? Couldn't He have made a lesser bad option than Hell? Sure, but that would necessarily mean there would have to be a lesser good option for Heaven as a result. Like darkness and cold, which are defined by the absence of light and heat, Hell is defined by the absence of God. But, if Hell is the absence of God, couldn't those who are living on earth right now without Him be experiencing Hell now? Even though many do not choose Him now, His presence is still here. So when they die and are "no longer on this earth," they are once and for all separated from His presence. And as I said, He just gives us what we have been asking for all along. He is a gentleman/woman or, well, you get it. He gives us what we have asked for! And since He is also light, those who don't choose to be with Him are left in utter darkness! Sorry, it's not a crazy party with all your rowdy friends. It's darkness – utter darkness. That freaks me out a little bit.

And while He is a God of justice, I believe He takes no pleasure, and in fact experiences significant pain, when the consequences of our poor decisions are meted out. Dads of teenagers, you totally understand what I'm talking about right now don't you!? He is both a God of intense love and of unmitigated wrath. "For the wrath of God is revealed from heaven against all ungodliness and unrighteousness of men, who by their unrighteousness suppress the truth." (Romans 1:18 ESV) Because He is just, we just don't get the loving, uplifting, forgiving, sustaining, patient God-of-the-second (third, fourth, and fifth) chance, and not get the avenging, vengeance-taking, hell-fire-raining, earth quaking, ocean rebuking God of Heaven's armies along with it. He is the comforter and counselor, and He is the judge and executioner. If *that* is not a dichotomy, I'm not sure what is!

I think more often than not, we see Him as the latter. All too often in movies and books, like Darren Aronofsky's recent film *Noah*, the version we get from the culture is the angry, punishing God who is responsible somehow for all of our woes, and who exacts ritualistic obedience through terror and calamity. Yes, He is really, really big and stronger than anyone or anything. But we quickly gloss over His more father-like, patient, forgiving attributes because, well, that side of Him just doesn't grab the headlines. Yet, the scriptures are riddled with accounts of Him displaying what can only be described as human emotion.

- Anger – Psalm 7:11; Deuteronomy 9:22; Romans 1:18
- Laughter – Psalm 37:13; Psalm 2:4; Proverbs 1:26
- Compassion – Psalm 135:14; Judges 2:18; Deuteronomy 32:36
- Grief – Genesis 6:6; Psalm 78:40; Isaiah 68:10
- Love – 1 John 4:8; John 3:16; Jeremiah 31:3
- Hate – Proverbs 6:16; Psalm 5:5; Psalm 11:5
- Jealousy – Exodus 20:5; Exodus 34:14; Joshua 24:19
- Joy – Zephaniah 3:17; Isaiah 62:5; Jeremiah 32:41

Read more: http://www.gotquestions.org/does-God-have-emotions.html#ixzz2xsBuloIi[16]

Where did we think *our* emotions came from? To have the full gambit of emotions, we had to have gotten them from some place.... How about being facetious? Is God sometimes facetious? He sometimes throws things out there that cause us to scratch our heads. God "personifies" Himself saying to Moses, "Leave me alone so my fierce anger can blaze against them (Israel after the golden calf incident), and I will destroy them. Then I will make you, Moses, into a great nation." (Exodus 32:10 NLT) Okay, so God knew He wasn't going to do any such thing, so why does He throw this out there—for dramatic effect? He demonstrates surprisingly human emotion in His exasperation and frustration with Israel. Just leave me alone, I'm gonna whack them! And you, my only good boy, you and I will go on, and I just won't have to deal with that rabble anymore! The ungrateful snots! (DKJV)

He is an emotional Father who can no more stomach my lousy destructive decisions than my dad could, who, when I was sixteen years old, still bent me over his knee and spanked my butt for acting like a... well, a three-year-old. I try to think back now and remember what was going through my head when I was doing pretty much everything that I knew my parents didn't want me to. I wasn't rebellious, just sneaky. Walking through the teen years with my daughters, I made multiple calls to my parents, apologizing for the torment that I put them through. I honestly have not felt anguish anything like the magnitude of what I felt over my daughter flatly rebelling against me. Many sleepless nights, I stared at the ceiling, wondering how any being could handle that feeling day after day after day! Armed combat was nothing compared to the gut-wrenching horror of the idea that I was "losing" my daughter and she, losing her soul. In combat I at least had control of a few things, and if I died, I guessed I could handle that. But flesh of my flesh, my baby (they hate that), lost? I'd rather it be me.

He feels that all the time. He is, after all, a Father. I handed over my eldest daughter in marriage recently. The year leading up to the wedding was, tumultuous. Lots of late night heart-to-heart, intense sort of conversations with my "baby girl," who was no longer a baby and soon no longer to be mine. Okay, that is a bit overdramatic, but guys, it is – again – a heart-rending thing to "give your daughter away." Wrestling with their rebellious sides (some of them more pronounced than others), struggling over their pulling away from my leadership and from my home, and their insistence that I allow them to … be … free, takes its toll. And

I am only left standing there to pay the bill. Dude, God has every right to be angry if He wants to be! I certainly would be – all the stinking time! Who would choose to be a father if he knew beforehand (had fore-knowledge) that it would cost him his heart!?

God, at some point, had to have stood at that crossroads, thinking, "If I go ahead and create them, they are going to rip out my heart and hate, steal, kill – disobey. But it is still worth it if just a few would love Me." When the light of that thought dawned on me, I nearly fell over–like onto my knees, in awe and wonder. What a wreck we must make of His heart. He is, after all, a Father.

"We can only worship someone we love. And we can only love someone we know." – David Jeremiah

"No one has ever seen God. But the unique One, who is himself God, is near to the Father's heart. He has revealed God to us." (John 1:18 NLT)

"But you may not look directly at my face, for no one may see me and live." (Exodus 33:20 NLT)

Versus

Jesus answered: "Don't you know me, Philip, even after I have been among you such a long time? Anyone who has seen me has seen the Father. How can you say, 'Show us the Father'?" (John 14:9)

Chapter 10

NOW YOU SEE HIM NOW YOU DON'T

We can't see Him, but we have seen Him? If we look Him in the face we won't survive it? (Exodus 33) I and the father are One, and look Me in the eye, touch My hands, feel the spot in My side where the spear was thrust...? (Luke 24) I can see where folks might get a little confused. But the confusion is – I believe – purposeful. If you have no interest in understanding the truth about Him, or if you have an interest in disproving what the Bible does say about you (so that you can sleep at night), then it is easy to stand at a distance and throw stones at divergent statements like this.

On the surface, they may seem to contradict one another. However, if you are willing to dig a bit deeper, to take a harder look at what is really going on, to wrestle, then there is much, much more in those words than you realize. That is the thing about scripture. Everyone inside the Church says to read it, and so we give it a surface level skimming and things like this seem to flatly contradict each other. And we just write it off as a misunderstanding. But you know that there is more going on there. We just don't want to take the time to dig in a little and see what the "more" is. It may take a little effort, a little work. But I am telling you, there is a veritable treasure trove of very cool ideas and understanding just below the surface of what you think you do not understand when scripture bumps up against itself like this. I promise you, if you dig a little into the scriptures and make an honest effort to understand what is being conveyed, you will be richly rewarded for your efforts!

Are you willing to dig? Are you willing to wrestle? Consider, for example, the Trinity. You know, God the Father, God the Son, and God the Holy Ghost. Wrapping our brains around the whole concept of the Trinity is difficult at best. But understanding at least the principle (one What and three Whos) gives us a place to start. Honestly, anyone who tells you they have the whole Trinity deal completely figured out, is either really deluded or supremely arrogant, and in either case you should run the other way. For a human being to claim to have completely defined a concept as simple-yet-complex as the Trinity, and say he has the only authoritative interpretation, is ridiculous. So we wrestle with three separate people and one entity... see, I'm struggling just with a simple analogy.

Theologians shudder and like to poke holes in the portrayal of the Trinity in Wm Paul Young's The Shack, but I kind of dig it! And before those who think Young is a heretic start freaking out, consider that in my small, finite, simple, third grade mind (... unless you change and become like little children you will never enter the kingdom of heaven...), I find his word pictures – albeit fiction – highly palpable and even comforting in that they resonate with my own experience of a personal relationship with the God of the universe. Remember Jacob? Remember the wrestling? It's what He wants! Not dogma, a relationship! Give and take! Interesting exchanges, like those that I see depicted in Young's story. THAT was the other awesome thing that Jesus did on the cross! Before Jesus, getting an audience with God was ridiculous! I know this gets long, but that's the point! Check out what Israel had to do in order to go before God – before Jesus came:

Within the Holy Place of the tabernacle, there was an inner room called the Holy of Holies, or the Most Holy Place. Judging from its name, we can see that it was a most sacred room, a place no ordinary person could enter. It was God's special dwelling place in the midst of His people. During the Israelites' wanderings in the wilderness, God appeared as a pillar of cloud or fire in and above the Holy of Holies. The Holy of Holies was a perfect cube — its length, width and height were all equal to 15 feet.

A thick curtain separated the Holy of Holies from the Holy Place. This curtain, known as the "veil," was made of fine linen and blue, purple and scarlet yarn. There were figures of cherubim (angels) embroidered onto it. Cherubim, spirits who serve God, were in the presence of God to demonstrate His almighty power and majesty. They also guarded the throne of God. These cherubim were also on the innermost layer of covering of the tent. If one looked upward, they would see the cherubim figures.

The word "veil" in Hebrew means a screen, divider or separator that hides. What was this curtain hiding? Essentially, it was shielding a holy God from sinful man. Whoever entered into the Holy of Holies was entering the very presence of God. In fact, anyone except the high priest who entered the Holy of Holies would die. Even the high priest, God's chosen mediator with His people, could only pass through the veil and enter this sacred dwelling once a year, on a prescribed day called the Day of Atonement.

The picture of the veil was that of a barrier between man and God, showing man that the holiness of God could not be trifled with. God's eyes are too pure to look on evil and He can tolerate no sin (Habakkuk 1:13). The veil was a barrier to make sure that man could not carelessly and irreverently enter into God's awesome presence. Even as the high priest entered the Holy of Holies on the Day of Atonement, he had to make some meticulous preparations: He had to wash himself, put on special clothing, bring burning incense to let the smoke cover his eyes from a direct view of God, and bring blood with him to make atonement for sins.

"But only the high priest entered the inner room, and that only once a year, and never without blood, which he offered for himself and for the sins the people had committed in ignorance." (Hebrews 9:7)

Tradition states that the high priest's attendants would actually tie a rope around the ankle of the high priest so that in the event that there arose some 'issue' while he was in the presence of God, and he were to drop dead, he could be dragged out of the Most Holy Place! Thereby, it would not be defiled, and another could go in to atone for the sin of the people! Wow!!

Continuing with *The Tabernacle Place*:

So the presence of God remained shielded from man behind a thick curtain during the history of Israel. However, Jesus' sacrificial death on the cross changed that. When He died, the curtain in the Jerusalem temple was torn in half, from the top to the bottom. Only God could have carried out such an incredible feat because the veil was too high for human hands to have reached it, and too thick to have torn it. (The Jerusalem temple, a replica of the wilderness tabernacle, had a curtain that was about 60 feet in height, 30 feet in width and four inches thick.) Furthermore, it was torn from top down, meaning this act must have come from above.

As the veil was torn, the Holy of Holies was exposed. God's presence was now accessible to all. Shocking as this may have been to the priests ministering in the temple that day, it is indeed good news to us as believers, because we know that Jesus' death has atoned for our sins and made us right before God. The torn veil illustrated Jesus' body broken for us, opening the way for us to come to God. As Jesus cried out "It is finished!" on the cross, He was indeed proclaiming that God's redemptive plan was now complete. The age of animal offerings was over. The ultimate offering had been sacrificed.

We can now boldly enter into God's presence, "the inner sanctuary behind the curtain, where

143

Jesus, who went before us, has entered on our behalf." (Hebrews 6:19-20)

"Therefore, brothers, since we have confidence to enter the Most Holy Place by the blood of Jesus, by a new and living way opened for us through the curtain, that is, his body ...let us draw near to God with a sincere heart in full assurance of faith." (Hebrews 10:19-22)[17]

Did you hear that? What an awesome privilege! We can now "draw near to God" and actually enter into the Holy of Holies – that is, we can now have a personal audience and a personal relationship with Him, the King, and yet our Daddy (Abba as Jesus put it). But I digress...

So if He says we can't look directly at His face, clearly that means something more is going on if He also says we have seen Him in Jesus. You can get all hung up on the Trinity in this instance, but the point is, you are not looking the first Person of the Trinity in the face when you look at Jesus. He did this a few other times in scripture–put on human skin. When those three dudes meet with Abraham (Gen 18:2), when our boy Jacob wrestles with some guy all night (Gen 32:24-30), and again in Gen 12:7, and other places,

God actually appears. A name has even been given to His appearing in this way, "Theophany." God puts on human skin. Why? Because if He didn't, we would not survive the encounter – like He said. Pillars of fire, burning bush, clouds, doves, three guys, one guy, we are left to fill in the details of how, when, and where He appears, but that also leaves room for argument.

It is in that space that so many of us get tangled up claiming, "No, this is how God is – No, THIS is how He is – Is not! – Is so! – Is not, is not, is not...." See, there's that third grader showing himself again! That is why we have so many different takes on exactly who and how God is! That's why there is going to be struggle – both with each other, and with Him. Precisely by *not* splitting the skies and coming down and ending all the arguments, He incites the struggle. And here, as I see it, is the purpose for the struggle: when we don't get all the answers we are looking for, or at least not the ones we expect, THAT is when faith enters in. It is at that point that our ***relationship*** with Him supersedes our understanding! Remember, the third option in the argument over what has purposely been left vague? In upside down world, He seems just that casual about the very thing that is the cornerstone of our relationship with Him – faith. Paraphrasing Andy Stanley in <u>Deep & Wide</u>:

Faith, or trust, is at the center of every healthy relationship. As trust goes, so goes the relationship. A break in trust signals a break in the relationship. A choice not to trust is what broke the relationship in the first place – thanks Adam! Just as that relationship was destroyed by a lack of faith, so it can be restored through an expression of the same. At its core, Christianity is an invitation to reenter a relationship of trust with the Father.[18]

With so much riding on faith, why the enticement and the invitation to wrestle? After all, the potential fallout from wrestling and losing is the possibility that we would just walk away. Yet, He chooses to take that risk! If I had the power to *make* my kids obey everything I told them to do, would I be so gracious, or wildly risk taking? God wants us to have life-altering faith on one hand, faith that not only believes, but acts. On the other hand, He expects us to continue to wrestle and never settle – to continuously "test the spirits." (1 John 4:1) As C.S. Lewis illustrated in the climax of his Narnia series, we simply can never come to the end of Him. There will always be "further in and further up" to climb.

To continue climbing and continue wrestling and yet trust in His provision is itself a dichotomy of sorts. But that is what He expects. The parable of the talents helps illustrate this (Matthew 25:14-30): don't take what I have given you and go dig a hole and bury it! Use what I have given you to dig even deeper and discover more about Me–which will reveal more about you, how I have wired you, and what I have made you to do! The gift is not for you to sit there and hold. If we just sit back on our haunches and declare that "what will be will be" because He is sovereign, we are missing out and missing the point.

The acts, "works", or "deeds" He speaks about in James 2:26 are the actions or behavior that we engage in–they are what comes out of us as a result of our wrestling and getting to know Him. Those "works" may well be part of the wrestling itself. But the investing of our lives and talents in the lives of others–the sharing of our experiences in the midst of the struggles so that others may benefit, is definitely something He intends for us to do…. The skin He may want to put on just might be yours! The secret hidden-in-plain-site treasure, the mystery discovery that changes everything, is the little known (or unacknowledged) truth that we were all unknowingly hard-wired for service! Though it doesn't sound like a 'Rocking Awesome Adventure!!!', think about the things that you have done that gave you the greatest feeling of connection and just made you feel... ... good, as you stepped away. You know, an honest, hard day's work. Or that time when you did something that significantly helped someone else, maybe at some cost to you, but it could never be paid back. Usually, these moments involve sacrificing time and/or treasure, and often they have something to do with *others*. Interesting that we are born screaming for comfort and for some of us, all our lives are spent scratching and clawing away for more– for ME! 'Me' so easily becomes the center of the universe, and all my efforts become one big 'me' love fest! Don't get me wrong, there is nothing wrong at all with taking care of yourself, but narcissism has suddenly become en vogue! And this tendency actually pulls us in the polar opposite direction of the very thing that we were made for–the very thing that, if we were to give it the same time and effort we give to pleasing ourselves, would blow our minds with a joy so full that it would overwhelm us!

Imagine a drug that is highly addictive, yet also has fantastic health benefits! Being used by God in the manner for which you were designed, using the talents and skills that are most familiar and enjoyable to you – that is the secret treasure! As with everything in life it seems, recognizing it and laying hold of it are just not quite that simple. We first have to believe that the treasure actually exists and in faith, without seeing it, go after it with reckless abandon!

There is a scene near the end of *Indiana Jones and the Last Crusade* – probably the most over-referenced scene of all time by those teaching on faith – where Indiana's father has been shot and is dying on the floor of a cave leading to a huge crevasse. Across the crevasse is another cave that houses a room full of counterfeit grails and also the one supposed Holy Grail, the cup Jesus drank from at the Last Supper. If he is able to get the one Holy Grail and if his father drinks from it, it will heal him, so the story goes. Problem is, there is a twenty-foot-wide gulf between the caves entrances. The notes in Indy's father's secret book of clues tell him that the only way to cross the divide is with a "step of faith." There appears to be no way across other than to step off the ledge and, in faith, expect something to stop him from falling. After laboring over the possible meanings of the clue, and hearing his father groan, "Indy, you must believe…" he closes his eyes and steps off into the abyss, only to have his foot strike an invisible bridge! The rock-colored and camouflaged footbridge is undetectable to the eye – but it is there. All the evidence and the clues point him in that direction, but the final step takes–faith.

So why do you suppose He has made it that way? Why is faith such a big deal? He showed Himself and tons of miracles to the disciples, whom we are supposed to emulate. But when was the last time you saw Him heal a blind man? He even went so far as to tell them, "You believe because you have seen me. Blessed are those who believe without seeing me." (John 20:29 NLT) That would include all of us–who believe. It's not like He is elusive. He says, "You will seek me and find me when you seek me with all your heart." (Jeremiah 29:13) Kind of a big qualifier there, "…when you seek me with all your heart." To those who are frustrated because they just haven't seen or heard Him act in their lives, you may be revealing more about the condition of your heart than you care to tell. You just can't fake it to a God who sees your heart. It really is an all or nothing deal to Him. He can't stand half-hearted, divided, one-foot-in-the-world, lukewarm people. Safe, easy, and well-preserved is not how He wants us to live–or die.

Not sure where this came from, but I love this idea: "Life is not about arriving at the grave safely and in a well-preserved body, but rather to skid in sideways in a cloud of smoke, used up, worn out, thrashed and out of breath, screaming, "Wow! What a ride!" Okay, so that is a little of my own commentary on life, but He does want all of us. He gave us life to be spent, expended, used, not selfishly kept to ourselves. Don't you want to be used to accomplish great things? Well, great things will necessarily involve others. Remember, in upside down world, greatness is servanthood. Step off that cliff in faith!

It's like repelling! If you have ever experienced the thrill of stepping off of a sheer cliff, or tower, or building, while roped into a climbing rope and gear, then you know that the fun doesn't start until you step off! You can stand there and stress all day. It is, after all, a bit unnatural to step off the edge of something that is really high up! You can say, "Nope!" and climb back down. You can take no risks. But you'd be missing out! Walking, bounding, floating, roping down that cliff face is awesome, empowering, and really just a lot of fun! So, step off!

Hebrews 11:6 says that without this faith, it is impossible to please God! But, 1 Corinthians 13:2 says that if I had faith enough to move mountains, but didn't love others, I would be nothing! So, does that mean that I could please God, but still be a nothing? That's still pretty good, isn't it!? Yes, but that is not what I was made for. Again, if I stop there, I'm missing out on the real fun! I will have climbed all the way to the edge of that cliff only to turn around and walk back down. Likewise, if I really do believe Him, then I won't stop at faith. I will act. I will do what He has asked me to do – helping and caring for others ahead of myself is a good place to start.

Say I were to fall off that cliff (without the rope). And as I topple over the edge I reach back and snag a root hanging out the side of the precipice. Now this smallish root is the only thing between me and a 300-foot drop to the rocks. As I start screaming for help, I hear this voice, "Darin, it's God, let go and I will catch you." What action would my faith produce? That's what you call a crisis of belief! "Is there anybody else there!?"

Faith cuts straight to that same issue that God is constantly testing us about. Faith is a "gut check" for what is *really* in your heart! I can say and do things all day long – show up at church, read my devotions, go to Bible study, and even serve on a mission team, but when the proverbial rubber meets the road, my actions Monday through Saturday will demonstrate the true state of my faith. My actions when it comes time to write the tithe check, hear the cancer diagnosis, lose my job, or let go of that root, will show what's truly going on inside. If my heart behind the things I say or do is just to impress myself and others, I will fail such testing. However, if my heart is settled in this relationship, in this faith that God is so concerned about, then the next steps in times of crisis are as simple and as natural as going to the sink for a glass of water, or like running back to the arms of my Father, who had just dislocated my hip! Now *that* is a dichotomy!

Which takes us back to the desert!

After the all-night scrap with God, Jacob comes away wounded, but alive. He is also blessed! Part of the blessing he received was the struggle itself. Even so, things don't get much easier for Jacob from that point. The locals violate his daughter, his wife Rachel dies, his relationship with his brother does not improve much and Esau eventually moves away, and he walks with a limp because his hip is messed up! But in spite of all of the turmoil, it is clear that things are different. The change in his name from Jacob (which means, "he grasps the heel," or "he deceives") to Israel (meaning, "he struggles with God" or "God prevails") is evidence of a remarkable transformation. He is no longer running away from difficulties. Instead, he runs headlong *into* them. He isn't the ineffectual conflict avoidance wimp he had been. He has an air of confidence – not merely in himself, but in God! He is bulletproof.

Why the change? Well, the blessing of course. It didn't look much like a blessing I suppose with him gimping around all the time. He didn't just get something from God – an answer to a question, more stuff, peaceful coexistence with his brother. All of the struggling leading up to that point and all that followed were working together to bring Jacob to the end of himself. Up until that point, his posturing and his conniving and his own strength had gotten him by. "*After the encounter, Jacob limped on his hip* [for the rest of his life], *each step reminding him that he no longer operated in his own strength, but in God's.*"[19] You'd think we could figure this out ahead of time, before circumstances drive us to our knees. But all too often, it is not until that point that we, like Jacob, seeking refuge from our terrible circumstances, grab on desperately. Why do we have to come to the end of ourselves before we will earnestly, desperately, honestly, finally scream for help?!

An unfeeling, disassociated, calculated, detached God who predetermined all of our circumstances would not care and would not be moved. But, a God who, more than anything else, wants a relationship with us, who longs to be remembered and involved in every part of our lives, will not simply show up, "split the skies with a Cecil B. DeMille effect (a la *Transformers 3* technology), and suddenly just appear." Instead, He allows difficulty and strife, and even unbelief to tweak us into questioning Him.[20] He says things like "don't kill"(Exodus 20:13), and "I regret that I ever made them."(Genesis 6:7) He builds into our DNA a homing beacon that, somewhere in the depths of our minds, deep in our bones, points to Him. Then, He gives us just enough information about Himself, and just enough evidence to help us see our need for Him. And He makes an offer to every single one of us–to wrestle!

ENDNOTES

[1] Michael Shurtleff, *Audition* (NY: Bantum, 1980), 25, 29.

[2] David Jeremiah, *Turning Point Radio*, (2014), Retrieved from:

http://www.davidjeremiah.org/site/radio.

[3] Francis Scott Key, The Star Spangled Banner (lyrics), 1814, MENC: The National Association for Music Education National Anthem Project. Retrieved September 14, 2007.

[4] Steve Collins, Christian Faith and Military Service, 2006,(Sioux Falls, SD) http://stevenmcollins.com/html/military_service.html.

Read everything Steve has to say about military service and Jesus! He has some very well thought out points. Then go read everything he has to say about the Lost Tribes of Israel!

[5] Dean, Paul. Reno, Mike. Frenette, Matt. Everybody's working for the weekend. "Working for the Weekend". Get Lucky. Vinyl. Epic/Sony. 1981

[6] James Prather; https://thinkhebrew.wordpress.com/2009/12/22/the-withering-fig-tree/#more-799

[7] David Jeremiah, *The Jeremiah Study Bible*, 2013, (Brentwood, TN: Worthy Publishing); Pg 1299 notes on Matthew 10:34

[8] C Michael Patton, *Reclaimingthemind.org*, What Happened To The Twelve Apostles? How Their Deaths Evidence Easter, April 10th, 2009

www.reclaimingthemind.org/blog/2009/04/what-happened-to-the-twelve-apostles-how-their-deaths-evidence-easter/.

[9] James C. Dobson, *When God Doesn't Make Sense*, 1993, (Carol Stream, IL: Tyndale House Publishers); excerpt from http://www.drjamesdobson.org/articles/voice-you-trust/god-always-makes-sense

[10] www.Bible.org

1. Irenaeus and Tertullian:
   a. Image — physical aspects of humanity
   b. Likeness — spiritual aspects of humanity
2. Clement of Alexandria, Origen, Athanasius, Hilary, Ambrose, Augustine, and John of Damascus
   a. Image — nonphysical characteristics of man
   b. Likeness — aspects of man that can be developed such as holiness or morality, and if not developed then are lost.
3. The Scholastics (Thomas Aquinas)
   a. Image — mankind's rational ability and freedom (natural)
   b. Likeness — original righteousness and supernatural gifts that were lost at the fall.

4. The Reformers
    a. All basically denied any distinction between the terms (Gen. 5:1; 9:6).
    b. Luther and Calvin both express this concept in different terms, but basically express the same truth
5. I think that they refer to our (1) personality; (2) consciousness; (3) language skills; (4)volition; and/or (5) morality.

[11] Andy Andrews, *The Butterfly Effect*, 2009, (Kansas City, MO: Hallmark Gift Books, 2011), 10-57.

[12] Paul Harvey Jr., *The Rest of the Story,* 1980-1981, (New York, NY: Bantam Books, 1981), 5-6.

[13] Rob Bell, Nooma 004, *Sunday*, 2005, (Grand Rapids, MI: Zondervan).

[14] John Meachem, (2006):God and the Founders, *Newsweek*, Retrieved from: www.newsweek.com/god-and-founders-107639.

[15] 1 Samuel 15:24 now screams in my ears at the retelling of this story. "I have sinned. I violated the LORD's command and your instructions. I was afraid of the men and so I gave in to them." After that it didn't go well for Saul :(

[16] S. Michael Houdmann, *GotQuestions.org*.

[17] The Holy of Holies and the Veil, *the-tabernacle-place.com*, http://the-tabernacle-place.com/articles/what_is_the_tabernacle/tabernacle_holy_of_holies.

[18] Andy Stanley, *Deep & Wide*, 2012, (Grand Rapids, MI: Zondervan), p. 105.

[19] David Jeremiah, *The Jeremiah Study Bible*, 2013, (Brentwood, TN: Worthy Publishing) notes on Genesis 32:31, p. 48.

[20] I guess we shouldn't feel too badly about writing Him off. Israel did after just 400 years in Egypt, and it has now been over 2,000 years since He showed Himself to us that way—except that God had not left the Hebrews with the Holy Spirit *living inside* of them....